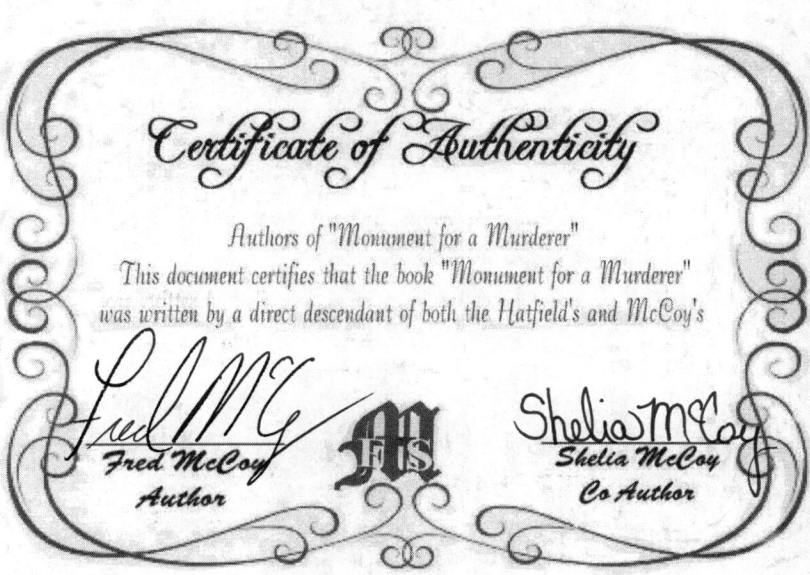

Certificate of Authenticity

Authors of "Monument for a Murderer"
This document certifies that the book "Monument for a Murderer" was written by a direct descendant of both the Hatfield's and McCoy's

Fred McCoy
Author

Shelia McCoy
Co Author

Dedication

This book is dedicated to:

Our children:

Ella Jane (McCoy) Schuler

Bobby Bryant McCoy

Hatfields and McCoys

Monument for a Murderer

"Americas Bloodiest Feud"

By: Fred & Shelia McCoy

"Monument for a Murderer"

Second Edition

All Rights Reserved

Copyright © 2012

By: Fred & Shelia McCoy

Reproduction in whole or in part without written permission is prohibited

Printed in USA

How to reach us:

Fred & Shelia McCoy 606-346-2198

hustpd@earthlink.net

fsmcy@windstream.net

www.fredmccoy.com

Read this book at your own risk it is (Rated X) for xciting. Authors are not responsible for temper flare ups, crying, fits of rage, and anger.

Special thanks to

My brother Barry McCoy

My Best Friend Paul Hatfield

Michael Hatter, Artist

Another great book

The Story of the McCoys

By Barry McCoy

THE FACTS, THE FEUD, THE FURY!

Randolph "Randall" McCoy

Written by a Descendant from both

The Hatfields and McCoys

"My Grandfather was a McCoy and his Mom was Preacher Anderson Hatfields daughter." – Barry McCoy

Order a copy of Barry McCoy's Book @

www.barrymccoy.com

Contents

Introduction	21
Genealogy	26
Logan Wildcats	28
Asa Harmon	30
Pig Trial	33
Election Day	38
Execution	44
Roseanna and Johnse	49
Sam McCoy kills Bill Staton	54
Cabin Massacre	58
Confessions of Charley Gillespie	65
Confessions of Ellison Hatfield	69
Battle of Grape Vine	71
Justice or Not	74
Devil Anse's Scapegoat	77
Last Hanging Ever in Pike County	80
"Ole" Randall McCoy	83
"Devil" Anse Hatfield	88
Sarah McCoy	93
"Preacher" Anderson Hatfield	98
"Judge" Wall Hatfield	100
"Bad" Frank Phillips	102
Perry Cline Esq.	106
Randall Saves Devil Anse's Life	109
Dave Stratton	111
The Real Hatfield Leader	112
Tolbert McCoy	114
Jim McCoy	116
Devil Anse's Legacy Continue	118
Governors at Odds	124
West Virginia Governor Bears Burden of Shame	127
Attempts to Kill Randall McCoy	128

Myths	132
Supreme Court	151
Monument for a Murder	155
Pattern of Behavior	160
Brother against Brother	162
Job	163
Book of Recommendation	165
Nicknames	166
Making a Mountain Out of a Mole Hill	168
Painful Memories	170
Practice What You Preach	171
Speak in Anger	172
If You Lay With Dogs You're Going to Get Fleas	173
Devil Tells True Story	174
Mr. Howell Replies Vigorously	176
The Gangs and Their Differences	178
Test Your Knowledge	179
Answers	185
Recipe for a Feud	189
TimeLine	190
Randall and Sarah McCoy's Children	193
Devil Anse and Levisa Hatfield's Children	194
Hatfield and McCoy Friends	195
Confederate Soldiers	197
Randall to be Victimized Again	198
Starving for Attention	201
In Closing	204
Credentials	207
Pictures	208
Father's Family Name	259
Credit/Disclaimer	260
Book Reviews	261
Pike County Tourism	262
Response to a Complaint	263
Who Won the Feud	265

Not an English teacher - just a cop

If you're looking for a book with perfect spelling, punctuation and grammar, this is not it. Being that this book was written, edited and published by direct descendants of the two feud families without the assistance of a professional editor or proof reader, you should not be surprise if it sounds a little "Hillbilly." After all, we are "Hillbillies," and proudly so. We suggest that when reading you do so while using a tad of tolerance for our "Hillbilly" language and grammar.

If, on the other hand, you're looking for some truths about the Hatfield and McCoy Feud, you'll find a lot of that between the covers of this book.

Doing the Right thing

Folks in the Tug Valley said the McCoys had nerves of steel, backbones the size of a fence post, and stubborn as an old rusted wagon wheel. Having known McCoys from as far back as my grandfather's generation, I can attest to the truth of the old saying. The old-time McCoys believed in two things God and the Justice System. If it had not been for Randall's and Sarah's love for God the feud could have been much worse. Sarah once said, she "Knew it was hard for Randall to go to Pikeville to court when he could just have easily gone the other way to Devil Anse Hatfield's house, but he did it for me and God."

No Apologies

At the start of this book we were digging out some Hatfield and McCoy, notes and heirlooms that have been passed down. Things that we have had packed away for years. Of course different family and friends said you're going to make some people mad at you. It is not our intent to make anyone mad, especially the Hatfield's or anyone who had ancestors associated with the feud. That's why it's taken so long for us to publish this book. The McCoys have never wanted to take the position of speaking out.

The feud took place over 148 years ago. It didn't involve anyone who is alive and breathing today. Since the news media wanted to dramatize the feud and with only one family talking, all we have to go by is the stories that were passed down over the years. I hope everyone reads this book with an open mind. It's not about the last names of two families; it's about right vs wrong, good vs bad, myth vs fact and life vs death. Some of the stories you may have heard before, but remember you were hearing Devil Anse Hatfield's version, and he was a conniving, kidnapping, murderer.

Do you think he could have been trusted to tell the truth? Read what I have heard and discovered over the years then do your own investigation and see which story to believe.

What I take issue with especially after being in Law Enforcement and the Criminal Justice System over half my life is the fact that Devil Anse Hatfield was never brought to justice. We want to reemphasize he was never held accountable.

The title of this book should have served as an indicator as to what our book is about. In Police work the title would be considered a "clue." Most people know when a family member does something wrong or embarrassing to the family name, we don't love them any less, but we know what they have done is wrong. Just as McCoys have talked about the feud over the years with each other, so have the Hatfields. I know this because I am related to both sides. Since I carry the McCoy name, I want to clear some things up. The bottom line is, Devil Anse Hatfield dramatically changed a lot of people's lives, **some he even ended.**

He lived a long life and grew to be an old man. He even repented, for his sins and for that we are glad. The Bible says, **"Obey the law of the Land,"** as well as **"thou shall not kill."**

Devil Anse did kill and he also had people killed. Now if he asks for God's forgiveness, I'm sure that since God is a merciful God, Devil Anse was forgiven. That doesn't change the fact that he was never held accountable for his crimes here on earth. The most horrendous of which was serial Capital Murder. After he claimed salvation and baptized, it would have been nice if he had climbed on old Fred (his horse) and rode to the Pike County Jail in Kentucky and turn himself in on the murder indictments that had been issued so many years earlier.

The purpose for writing this book is to contrast his long and prosperous life with the short lives of the young adults and children he killed, who never had the same opportunity to succeed in life that he had. Forget the last name, the famous feud and the monument; think for a moment of the atrocities for which this man was responsible. We know that this book is not going to change history as it has been presented, but we hope that the average person will leave this book with a better understanding of who this man everyone called "Devil" really was.

That old saying, "the truth will set you free," would have worked for Devil Anse. Had Devil Anse turned himself in and faced the charges he had eluded from for so many years, who knows with his age and political clout, they may have turned him loose. At least, he could have closed that chapter of his life by doing the right thing. Instead, he went down in history or at least in a lot of people's opinion as a murderer who was **"Above the Law."**

Jim Vance, Cap Hatfield, Johnse Hatfield, Judge Wall Hatfield, Cottontop Hatfield (Mounts) Elias Hatfield and all the others paid their debt according to the law of that day. Some of them served time in prison and some were even killed. The slain McCoys that the Devil murdered received no justice. We hope this book enlightens you to some facts you may not have known or just never looked at in a neutral and objective way as would a professional investigator.

An old saying befitting of the Feud

"A fool learns from his mistakes,
A wise man learns from the fool."

Preface

The direct descendants of the McCoys have commented publicly very little about the feud over the years. You could say those who know the most have talked the least.

Throughout the years, the McCoy ancestors have outright refused to talk to the media, reporters, authors, and outsiders in general about anything concerning the feud.

Some people believe that because the McCoys have failed or refused to talk to reporters, the facts have become cloudy or even non-existent. You might say the truth has become twisted or distorted. Maybe it made for a better story, but it wasn't the truth.

It's not about one family or the other. It's about the Truth and Justice. That's all Randall McCoy ever wanted. We can't give him Justice, but we can tell the truth as we heard it from our ancestors growing up on Blackberry Creek in Kentucky.

Please withhold your judgment and reach no opinion until the last word of this book is read.

Who Won the Feud?

A Note from the Authors

Everyone has a story. Between the covers of this book is ours, like it, hate it, agree or disagree, believe it or not, that's your right. After all this is America, land of the free, home of the brave. GOD Bless America.

This book consists of things that we know, stories that I was told and evidence we have investigated. This book is based on actual records of that time, speculation, rumors and any other resources we could find, including family stories that I heard over the years as a child growing up on Blackberry Creek where most of the feud took place.

This book is not like other books that have been written about the feud. What makes ours different is that I am a direct descendant of both the Hatfields and McCoys (see genealogy).

The McCoys and Hatfields were neighbors on the Kentucky side of the Tug River, and always got along well with each other. It was the West Virginia Hatfields-Devil Anse and his kin-who caused the troubles known as "The Feud."

In our opinions, these stories are as correct as we think they can be. Can we absolutely beyond a shadow of a doubt guarantee, they are one hundred percent true? NO! We do not believe that there has ever been a book published about the Hatfield and McCoy Feud that can say that, because no actual participant in the feud on either side ever wrote a book. As a famous man once said, "Believe it or Not, but it's our story."

The Hatfield and McCoy Feud was not the worst feud that West Virginia or Kentucky ever had. However, it was the bloodiest and most publicized. Some referred to it as a "private war" between two families instead of a feud.
The news media loved the drama caused by the feud. They helped to "fuel the fire" you might say. Their public loved reading about the two hillbilly families fighting over a love affair and a pig.

Most of the authors of Hatfield and McCoy books have gotten their stories from newspaper articles during that time. Since Randall McCoy, didn't talk to the news reporters you don't have to be Dick Tracy to figure out who was telling the stories. This means people have only been getting one side of the story throughout the years. That was Devil Anse Hatfield's side. Over the last 148 years, many people would ask questions of how something happened or if something was true or false that they had heard about the feud.

Since our McCoy, ancestors didn't talk; it put the McCoy's and their side at a disadvantage. All the books written to date seem to be favoring the Hatfield's side. The scales shouldn't be balanced by whom the author was, but by the truth. Let us reiterate when we talk about the Hatfield and McCoy Feud we want to be clear: It wasn't all the Hatfields, and it certainly wasn't all the McCoys feuding. In fact, history shows that some of the McCoys were on the Hatfield side, and some of the Hatfields were on the McCoys side. Some members of both families never got involved in the feud at all, and remained friends throughout the feud and the years following.

The feud basically stood between two men, Anse Hatfield and Randall McCoy. Both had large families, but neither leader had the full cooperation from all members of their respective families. A lot of the men on both sides just refused to get caught up in the chaos.

Being tagged with the famous name of McCoy has always been a conversation piece. Throughout the years people have asked who won the feud. I have always answered. If you want to know who lost the most family members in the feud it was the McCoys. If you want to know who had the best morals and respect for the law it was also the McCoys.

During this book when we refer to the Hatfields, we are in no way referring to the Hatfields of today or the Kentucky Hatfields of that time. We are referring to Devil Anse Hatfield and his followers of that time, who lived in West Virginia. As it was stated earlier there were some Hatfields and McCoys, who remained friends throughout the feud, some even married one another. (As did my Great Grandparents, Asa McCoy and Nancy Hatfield)

I don't think I'm revealing any big secret when I say Devil Anse was a cold blooded calculated murderer. In fact, I think he liked having that reputation. I think it re-enforced his already overzealous ego.

It is also a known fact that he was indicted by a Pike County Grand Jury for the kidnapping and murders of Randall McCoy's three sons. Let's forget the last names for now. It is a proven fact by the testimony at the trial that Devil Anse did, in fact, kidnap the three McCoy's from Kentucky Law

Enforcement Officers. Then two days later he tied them to trees and executed them in cold blood. It was also believed that Devil Anse ordered the killings of Randall McCoy and his family. These were capital crimes in Kentucky and crimes that Devil Anse was never held accountable for.

Now forget the famous feud and imagine these murders happening to your family and the perpetrator is at no time brought to justice. Forget the courts; the perpetrator was never even arrested for the crimes he was indicted for.

Now that should give you an idea of how Randall McCoy felt. He felt that way until the day he died. When I talk about Hatfields, I re-emphasize, I'm referring only to Devil Anse and his immediate family that orchestrated nothing less than devastation to the McCoy family. We live in a land where no one is above the law, with emphasis placed on Devil Anse Hatfield. If people feel they must honor Devil Anse, then at least honor him for his real accomplishments. "He murdered McCoys."

Let's call a spade a spade: he got away with murder. He did this at the sacrifice of his own children, brother, uncle and nephew, all of which were either killed, went to prison or were hung. I have wanted to speak out on the Devil Anse legacy since I was a child. However, since we were told as kids growing up "McCoy's don't talk about the feud," I had to remain silent. With the new interest in the feud if someone doesn't talk soon there will be no one left to refute the Myths. So I guess it's left up to my brother and I to tell what was passed down to us, and we are doing just that.

We wish people would research the facts instead of relying on a Hollywood movie that is only after high ratings.

After being a Police Officer for over half my life and always believing in the justice system it grieves me that such an injustice could have happened to my ancestors, in my home county. That a man could commit multiple murders and never be arrested does not set well with me, even when it does not involve my kin.

Most people thought Devil Anse deserved to be incarcerated or hung, rather than to be honored with a monument.

Introduction

"Our Story" about the Hatfield and McCoy, told as close to the truth as we know it.

The Good –The Bad – The Ugly.

For too many years we descendants, of the McCoy's have kept quiet and let others tell the story of the Hatfields and McCoy Feud. The McCoy family rarely talked of the feud, and never in public. It was a subject to avoid. As time heals all, tensions have eased over the years, through friendships, marriages and daily acquaintances.

Our family never talked to the media or book authors. As a result, they would get their information from whatever source they could. True or not it didn't matter as long as they got a story. The wilder the story the better they liked it. They would even take bits and pieces of information or rumors someone had heard and add whatever they needed in order to make it more appealing. It's not about one family or the other. It's about the TRUTH. I am frustrated by seeing misleading and one-sided accounts of things that did or didn't happen.

As far as I know there has never been a book where the authors are related to both the Hatfields and McCoys. Myself and my brother Barry McCoy, who has written his own book about the feud, are now correcting that situation. I have been a Police Officer for over 33 years. I think that qualifies me to investigate the facts and flaws of the feud. Who better to review these crimes and atrocities than a seasoned investigator and blood relative to both families?

Over the years, the McCoys have remained silent. This book and that of my brother will change that. By our McCoy ancestors not telling their story, we now have movies where Randall McCoy runs into trees drunk and cussing the very God he loved and honored even in the worst of times. It's time to tell the truth. It's time to correct the myths, and it's time to pass on what I, as an investigator and descendant, have learned from my investigations and what I was told growing up in feud country.

We mean no disrespect to either family name, but it's time to set the record straight. Being a direct decedent of both families I feel I have the right to attempt to correct some of the injustice that has been done to the McCoy name over the years and especially with the recent TV movie. All we can do is tell, "Our Story" you don't have to be a seasoned Police Officer to realize that some of the stories told over the years have been one sided.

It's the McCoys' own fault for not talking earlier and getting the facts out. However, with the marriages between the families no one wanted to make waves.

With each passing year, the feud would fade farther away, however with the most-recent Hatfield and McCoy movie it has brought the feud full circle. Now the younger descendants are asking if this is the way it really was. The older descendants try to explain, "Of course not!" The old saying "a picture is worth a thousand words" couldn't be truer. We doubt this book is going to have any great impact on removing the TV image of Randall McCoy cursing God, but we say it is a lie!

Nowhere in my life time have I or any of our ancestors ever been told that Randall or Sarah ever lost their faith in God. Their love for God was the very foundation that got them through such devastation in their lives.

I always heard what godly people Randall and Sarah McCoy were. In fact, even Devil Anse was attributed to calling Randall a just and Godly man (after Randall had saved Devil Anse's life during the war.)

The bottom line is that Randall McCoy was hurt at Devil Anse for leaving the war early, deserting, quitting, call it what you want, but the fact is Anse left the Army. With Devil Anse's reputation for violence back in the day there weren't a lot of people who would question him about anything negative, because they feared for their lives. He would have killed them. That was a proven fact.

Truth is Devil Anse left, and Randall stayed. No doubt Randall had it rough and felt guilty knowing his family probably needed him as much as Devil Anse's family needed their husband and father. However, Randall honored his commitment, and he kept his word.

Almost all the men in Randall's unit were killed, Randall along with my Great, Great Grandfather, Uriah McCoy, was taken Prisoner of War. Now he's really feeling hard towards a one-time friend, and it weighs on him as he sits in the prison camp. His family thinks he's dead. Times were already tough during this period, and now it got worse. With every passing day Randall realizes: I could have been working the fields; I could be out hunting game and helping to feed my family.

Then one day, by the grace of God, the war is over, and he's free to return to his home. He has pondered on the past so long sitting in a prison camp that it has scarred him. Upon returning home and seeing his family, Randall realizes they have suffered just as much as he has. He feels guilty he's been off fighting while his family has suffered so much in his absence. On the other hand, Devil Anse and his family are doing well. It's not a case of jealously as some have tried to portray. It is just a simple struggle with morals. Randall knowing he made a commitment to serve, honored that commitment, but by doing so it cost him his family and farm.

Soon after his arrival home he gets word that the Logan Wildcats have murdered his brother Asa Harmon McCoy. Most people have said this is what started the feud, but it was only another contributing factor that over time led to mayhem. The first offense was Devil Anse abandoning his post. Now Devil Anse or his men in the Logan Wildcats have killed Randall's brother.

On the occasion when Devil Anse and Randall did meet, Randall wasn't shy in speaking his mind. Randall had the kind of voice that carried, and he was known to talk loud. Some thought it was due to fighting in the war with guns and cannons going off so close to his ears. When they would meet and Devil Anse would try to make small talk, Randall wasn't interested and his question to Devil Anse was usually, "Why? Why did you leave?" Randall had lost all respect for him, and he wanted it to show, this really angered Devil Anse. It was an insult to his ego to be questioned on his ethics, moral and bravery.

It was common knowledge that Devil Anse was a natural-born leader, and the men counted on him. Of course after a couple of times of being asked this question and mostly in public, Devil Anse became embarrassed. His frustration grew into a total dislike of his one-time friend. To Devil Anse it was just intolerable to be admonished in front of anyone. He wanted to be larger than life to all who knew him and Randall, by speaking out boldly, was putting a damper on his reputation.

Genealogy

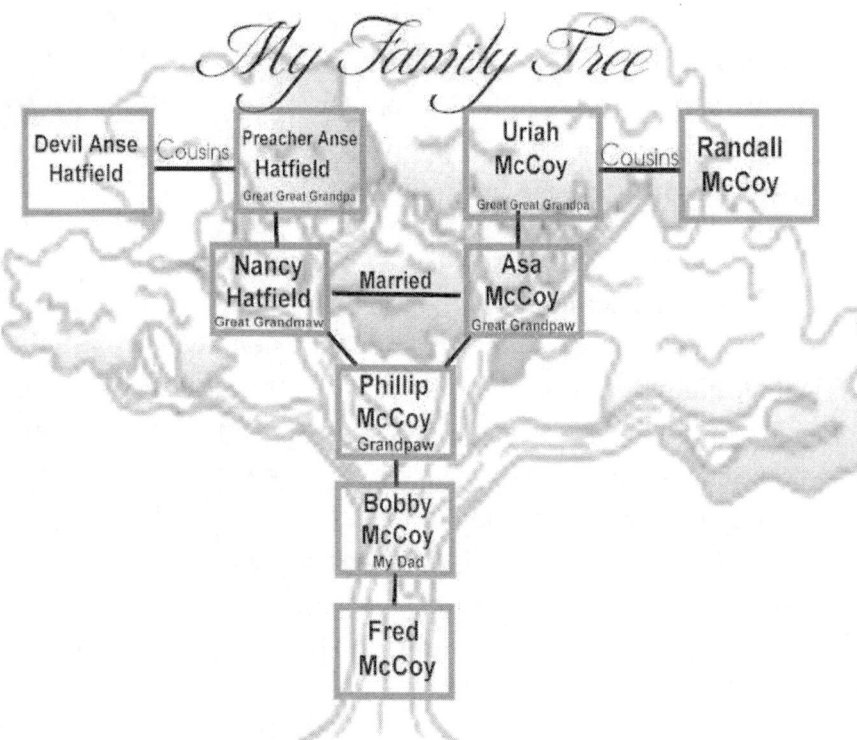

The chart above shows how I am related to both the Hatfields and McCoys. As you can see my Great Grandmother was Nancy Hatfield, daughter of "Preacher" Anderson Hatfield she married my Great Grandfather who was Asa McCoy *(named after Asa Harmon McCoy)*.

William McCoy 1750

1st McCoy recorded

| Daniel 1790 | brothers | Samuel 1782 |
| Randall 1825 | Cousins | Uriah 1827 |

My Great Grandfather- **Asa McCoy 1854**

My Grandfather- **Phillip McCoy 1890**

My Father- **Bobby McCoy 1932**

Me- **Fred McCoy 1958**

Fred and Shelia McCoy - Married April 13th 1985

Our children

Daughter Ella Jane (McCoy) Schuler 1986

Son Bobby Bryant McCoy 1987

Randall McCoy's father and my G.G. Grandfather Uriah McCoy's fathers were brothers

Logan Wildcats

Formed 1863

The Logan Wildcats were a band of armed irregulars led by Devil Anse Hatfield. They were active in Logan and Wyoming Counties. Devil Anse formed the confederate guerrilla fighting unit after him and his brothers, Lt. Ellison Hatfield, Private Elias Hatfield and their cousin Private Ephraim Hatfield all with the 45th Va. Inf. Battalion deserted the Confederate Army on or about Dec. 19th 1863 other members of the Logan Wildcats that were connected to the feud were as follows:

Devil Anse Hatfield, Ellison Hatfield, Elias Hatfield, Ephraim Hatfield, Johnson "Johnse" Hatfield, William "Cap" Hatfield, Wall Hatfield, Sam Mayhorn, Dock Mayhorn, Plyant Mayhorn, John Whitt, Tom Chambers, Charley Carpenter, Lark Varney, Andy Varney, Alex Messer, Selkerk McCoy, L.D. McCoy, Dan Whitt, Ellison (Cottontop Mounts) Hatfield, Charley Gillespie, Jim Vance.

These men were ruthless but persistent in hanging together at all cost. They were like the three musketeers, until the crap hit the fan then they would squeal like a "pig" on each other. (See confessions in another chapter). The Civil War started April 12th 1861 and ended April 9th 1865. Those who are listed above that were in the Confederate Army, deserted about the same time as Devil Anse and other family members. It was said that Devil Anse attempted to talk Randall and Uriah McCoy in to deserting and returning home with the rest of them, but they refused. Randall and my Great Great Grandfather would have loved to have gone home to their families, but they just couldn't desert the other men in their unit.

Asa Harman McCoy

Illustrated by Michael Hatter
Please do not copy these sketches without the written permission of Fred McCoy

What role did Asa Harman McCoy play in the feud? Asa was Randall's younger brother who in 1863 joined the North to fight in favor of the Union. While fighting he suffered an injury bad enough to be discharged and sent home. He returned to Pike County in 1864 only to receive unwarranted threats from the ruthless instigator Jim Vance. After hiding out in a cave for days at Bluespring, a small hollow on Blackberry Creek, Asa was murdered. The killer(s) was never named or brought to justice. It was thought Devil

Anse himself had murdered Asa Harmon but some say Devil Anse was home, sick that day and Jim Vance actually murdered him. Seeing as how we're attempting to deal only in facts with the writing of this book we will have to leave it to speculation.

There is no proof as to who actually pulled the trigger that fired the bullet that killed Asa Harmon McCoy. We do know that it was a member of the Logan Wildcats. What we also know is that even though Ole Ran'l was disappointed in Asa Harmon because he had joined to fight for the North, he was still devastated that Asa was killed and even more disappointed he was unjustly killed by Devil Anse's band of deserters and renegades. It weighed on him that he had once saved Devil Anse's life in battle and now he or one of his Wildcats had murdered his younger brother. It was unthinkable and inexcusable.

Even though Randall was not happy with Asa's decision to fight for the North, he didn't love his brother any less as clan pride and family loyalty were strong in the mountains. This was the first death of the feud, but since the Hatfield's had drawn first blood, surely more would follow. Author Note: I am not a fan of slavery, and if I was living back in the days of the Civil War, I too would have fought for the Union.

Asa Harmon- This is where he was killed by the Logan Wildcats.

Bluespring in Ransom, Kentucky, (near Blackberry Grade School) in Pike County.

Coordinates: 37° 33.461' N, 82° 11.505' W.

Pig Trial

Coordinates: 37° 34.815' N, 82° 10.803' W.

Marker is at the bottom of Blackberry Mountain, at the intersection of KY Hwy 1056 and KY 319

It was 1878; thirteen years after Harmon had been killed. The Civil war was over, and everyone had returned home. During this era, in order to prove ownership, it was customary for farmers to cut a recognizable "notch" out of the pig's ear. Then they would take a knife and carve "their mark" inside the inner lip of the pig's ear. (Usually their initials) Then they would bust a few poke berries and rub them into the cuts to create a permanent tattoo. Afterwards, they would just turn the pig loose to roam in the spring and summer. Then in the fall the farmers would send their children out to gather in their hogs for slaughter.

One autumn day when Ole Ran'l stopped by to visit Floyd Hatfield, who was the son of George Hatfield and a cousin to Devil Anse Hatfield. Randall's wife and Floyd's wife were sisters, which made Randall and Floyd brother n laws.

While Randall was visiting he noticed that Floyd Hatfield had one of his pigs in a lot beside of his barn on the hill as if he were trying to conceal it. Randall being a firm believer in the law took Floyd to court. Randall said, "It was not about the pig, but the accountability and justice being served." Randall also said that he would have given the pig to Floyd if he thought he was in need, but stealing it was another matter. When the trial finally came around, both families and several neighbors arrive at court to witness the outcome. Seated on the jury were six Hatfields and six McCoys.

Bill Staton, who was Ellison Hatfield's brother-in-law, was the only witness and many said he was dog drunk the day of the trial. Bill testified that the pig was Floyd Hatfield's. When it was time for the verdict, the six Hatfield's voted it was Floyd's pig, and five McCoy's voted it was Randall's pig. However, Selkerk McCoy, the sixth juror who worked for Devil Anse and was married to a Hatfield, voted it was Floyd Hatfield's pig. In the end, Floyd won the case.

Randall and many of the McCoys felt that Bill Staton and Selkerk McCoy were favoring the Hatfield's because of being married into the Hatfield family and to keep their jobs at the timber yard that was owned by Devil Anse. Randall considered the pig trial a travesty, with Bill Staton being a drunken witness, Selkerk and Bill being employed by the Hatfield's. The relationship between the Hatfields and McCoys would only worsen from this day forward.

      Randall knowing the pig was his became outraged that the justice system had somehow failed him. There was no doubt in his mind the pig bore the McCoy marking. However, Floyd said his family had already destroyed or shall we say devoured the pig in question. There was no physical evidence as to who really owned it. Randall asks why he didn't bring the marked ear to court as evidence. Circumstances would have been different if the pig's ear had been produced. The marking on Randall's pig was infallible. His pig's ear had a distinction like no other. After enduring the trail Randall had no other recourse except to stipulate that he maintained the pig in question was in fact his. Had the pig not had his mark on its left ear Floyd would have produced it in court.

      Many said that the pig was hanging in Floyd's smoke house and hadn't been eaten yet. A lot of people find it hard to believe that a pig had such an impact on the feud. In those days, such an offense was taken very seriously especially to a large family, hogs were extremely valuable and a great source of food.

(Appalachian Farmers used the poke berry juice as tattoo dye on their livestock.)

After taking a small knife and cutting the mark you wanted to use in the pigs inner ear, the farmer would then rub the poke berry juice into the cut which made a permanent tattoo in the pig's ear. **(See pic)**

You can see a "notch" cut out of pig's left ear with an M carved and tattooed into the ear using a knife and poke berries.

There's a big difference between an (H) and an (M)
Of course some just used the letter X some didn't use the tattoo at all only the notch due to being unable to write.

Note: No doubt the reason why the pig or the pig's ear was not introduced as evidence at the trial.

Hog Trial Site

In the fall of 1878, Randolph McCoy brought charges against Floyd Hatfield for stealing one of his hogs. The resulting trial occurred here and was presided over by the local justice of the peace, Preacher Anderson Hatfield. Preacher Anderson was Devil Anse Hatfield's cousin and did not want to appear biased so he gathered a jury of six Hatfields and six McCoys to hear the case. When the jury reached its verdict, Selkirk McCoy, nephew of Sarah McCoy and a veteran of the Virginia Confederacy, sided with the six Hatfields in favor of Floyd. The McCoys felt betrayed and open hostilities soon erupted between the Hatfield and McCoy families. Later Bill Staton, who testified in favor of his brother-in-law Floyd Hatfield, was killed by two of Randolph McCoy's nephews while he was hunting. They were tried and acquitted in a trial presided over by Valentine Hatfield, uncle of Devil Anse. After this, violence between the families continued and the resulting conflict eventually escalated into the most famous family feud in American history.

Coordinates: 37° 34.815' N, 82° 10.803' W.

Marker is in McCarr, Kentucky, in Pike County

Election Day

Murder or Self Defense?

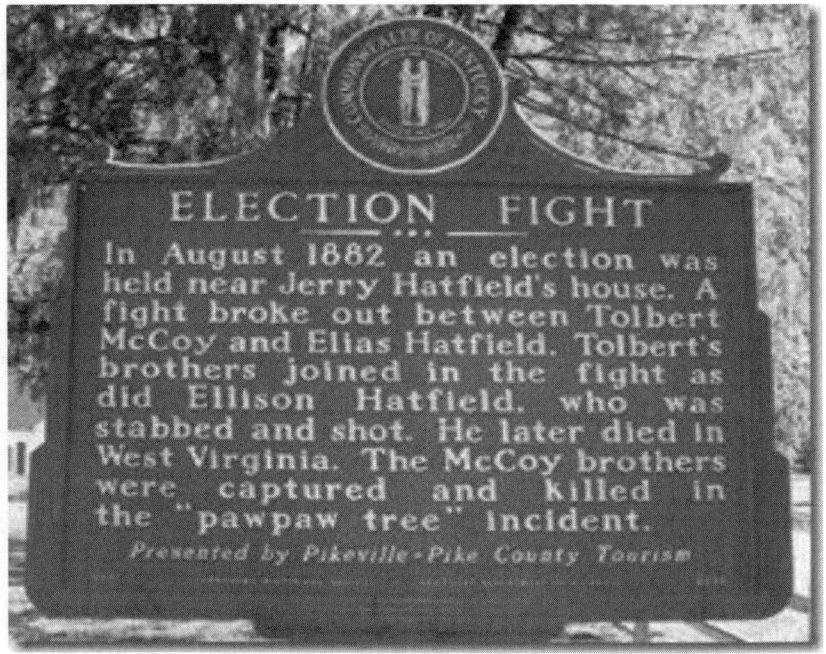

> **ELECTION FIGHT**
>
> In August 1882 an election was held near Jerry Hatfield's house. A fight broke out between Tolbert McCoy and Elias Hatfield. Tolbert's brothers joined in the fight as did Ellison Hatfield, who was stabbed and shot. He later died in West Virginia. The McCoy brothers were captured and killed in the "pawpaw tree" incident.
>
> *Presented by Pikeville-Pike County Tourism*

Coordinates: 37° 34.814' N, 82° 10.806' W.

Marker is in McCarr, Kentucky, in Pike County

    What does anyone really know about the Election Day Fight and Stabbing? We know it started off as any other election day with everyone getting together and socializing. It was a day for the women to trade recipes and gossip. It was like a major holiday or festival and especially in Pike County, Kentucky and Logan County, West Virginia people took elections seriously. Who knows? You might need a favor one day so you will want someone in office that will be there to return a favor for the vote you gave them.

There was abundance of food, people, and of course moonshine. Everyone knows some of the best moonshine in the world is made in Pike County, Kentucky.

There is an old saying **"many things can be preserved in alcohol; dignity is not one of them."**
There was song and dance, courting and games. Everyone always had a good time. This Election Day was no different, but it was all about to change.

There are stories, rumors, and even books over the years that have told stories as to what actually took place that day. Some say Elias Hatfield from West Virginia owed some money to Tolbert McCoy for a fiddle and refused to pay. Elias and Tolbert got into a fight, and Tolbert had whipped him pretty bad. Ellison saw the fight and asks Tolbert if he wanted to try that with him.

Some said there was still bad blood over the pig trial, and of course, everyone knew there was bad blood between Ellison and the McCoy's because he had filed false criminal charges on Sam and Paris McCoy. Then, there was the time when Tolbert was a Deputy Sheriff and had arrested Johnse Hatfield on Pike County warrants. There are just too many stories to list; they would complete a book themselves.

What is a fact is that Ellison started a fight with Tolbert when he told him "you're fix in' to get an ass kick in' boy" and swung at his head with a right fist. Then the fight was on, as it progressed each family was cheering for their own kin. In a matter of seconds, like any bar room brawl (without the bar), everyone was fighting. Crazy Jim Vance and

Jim McCoy, Cap Hatfield and Paris McCoy, Sam McCoy was fighting with Elias Hatfield.

Ellison was just a little over confident about his fighting ability. Tolbert gave him a run for his money; but ultimately Ellison had Tolbert on the ground and was hitting him with a large rock about the size of Ellison's fist. Pharmer saw what was going on and attempted to get Ellison off of Tolbert. With Ellison as big as he was and Pharmer only knee-high to a grass hopper, he wasn't much help. Tolbert pulled his knife from his pocket and began to stab Ellison in the gut.

According to eyewitness accounts that were actually there that day, Tolbert stabbed Ellison maybe six to seven times at the most. Pharmer saw that with Ellison being so big and Tolbert's knife being so small, it wasn't affecting Ellison in the least and fearing that Ellison was going to kill Tolbert, he yelled at Randall Jr. saying, "Ellison's killing Tolbert!" Randall Jr. ran to Ellison and tried to pull him off but even with both boys trying to pull Ellison it wasn't working. As a last resort, Pharmer pulls out a pistol, places it against Ellison's ribs on the right side, and shoots Ellison one time. Ellison fell to one side, and everyone just froze. Then Cap Hatfield yelled, "They shot Ellison!"

Contrary to all the stories that the three boys ran, they did not run. They thought it was self-defense they didn't really think they had done anything wrong. Since Ellison was beating Tolbert with a rock it was either let Ellison kill your brother or shoot Ellison. Pharmer and Randall Jr. went over to Tolbert, who was lying on the ground gasping for air with a huge 4-inch gash on top of his head and bleeding profusely.

Cannot confirm this is the rock used by Ellison Hatfield when attacking Tolbert McCoy. An old bridle and boot was used to demonstrate the size of the rock.

When the constable and his deputy who happened to be passing by the election ground heard the commotion, stopped and arrested the three McCoy boys.

Devil Anse hadn't been gone long when the fight broke out. He couldn't have been any more then 2-3 miles away. Tom Chambers jumped on his horse and rode off to catch up with him. He could have run in the Kentucky Derby as fast as he was running that day. He caught up with Anse just a little ways down the road. When he told Anse what had happened. Anse told Tom to trade his horse for the buckboard and take Levicey home. He mounted up and headed back to Blackberry.

By now, the constable had done left with the three McCoy boys and was headed towards the Pike County Jail. The McCoy's were unrestrained as well as non-combative. They in all sincerity thought they were justified in protecting Tolbert from serious injury or death, especially since Ellison was using a rock. They felt the charges were baseless as well as unjustified.

However, since they were the sons of law-abiding Randall McCoy, they knew to do what the Law said to do.

Right now, they are under arrest. They would just have to get it all sorted out in court or at least that's what they thought.

Devil Anse was almost back to the election grounds when he met the wagon hauling Ellison back to West Virginia. He stopped briefly to check on Ellison, then again, headed out to catch up with the McCoy's. By looking at Ellison, he knew Tom Chambers had not exaggerated when he told Devil Anse "it looks really bad." He wanted to catch up to the McCoy's before they reached the Pike County Jail.

Preacher Anse knowing that Devil Anse was going to be out of control told the Constable to "Get the boy's on out of here and into the jail before Anse gets back." When Devil Anse got to the election grounds, he was told the boys had been taken to the Pike County Jail. Preacher Anderson Hatfield asks Devil Anse to go home and take care of Ellison. Let the Law handle the McCoys. That would have been too easy for Devil Anse. Preacher Anse forgot who he was talking to. This is Devil Anse Hatfield; it was his way or the highway. Devil Anse looked at Preacher Anse and said I ain't got time to listen to you right now, Preacher. I have got to catch up to them McCoys. He took off towards Pikeville. In the meantime Wall Hatfield; Devil Anse's brother, Cap Hatfield, Johnse Hatfield, Crazy Jim Vance, and several more mounted up and followed after Devil Anse.

The Constable hadn't even reached Turkey Foot Gap when Devil Anse and the others caught up to them. Devil Anse asked the Constable what he was doing, and he replied, "taking these boys to the Pike County Jail." too which Devil Anse said "The hell you are. Those boys are coming with me." The Constable seemed to be getting ready to debate the matter with Devil Anse when Judge Wall Hatfield pulled his 45 cal. colt and said, "This is a non-debatable subject. We're taking the McCoys." They did just that, returning to West Virginia where they would stay for two days. After Ellison died, they returned the three boys to the river bank on the Kentucky side of the Tug River.

People always ask what Devil Anse, Ellison, Cap and the other West Virginia Hatfield's were doing at a Kentucky Election anyway. They couldn't vote for anything, and none of them had property in Kentucky.

None of the McCoys ever went to West Virginia when they were having elections. It wasn't good enough that Devil Anse ruled Logan County, West Virginia; now he wanted to rule Pike County, Kentucky as well.

Why not just let the Justice System take its course? If the boys were guilty, then put them in jail or hang them but don't take the law into your own hands. Then again, this was Devil Anse and he could do whatever he wanted to, or so he thought.

After what happened at the election grounds it wasn't surprising that the McCoys became teetotalers. They had seen first-hand how the moonshine had affected Ellison and Elias, and the outrages conduct it manifested. No doubt had Ellison Hatfield or Tolbert McCoy not had been inebriated, they may have done some things differently.

Execution

Of "The Real McCoy"

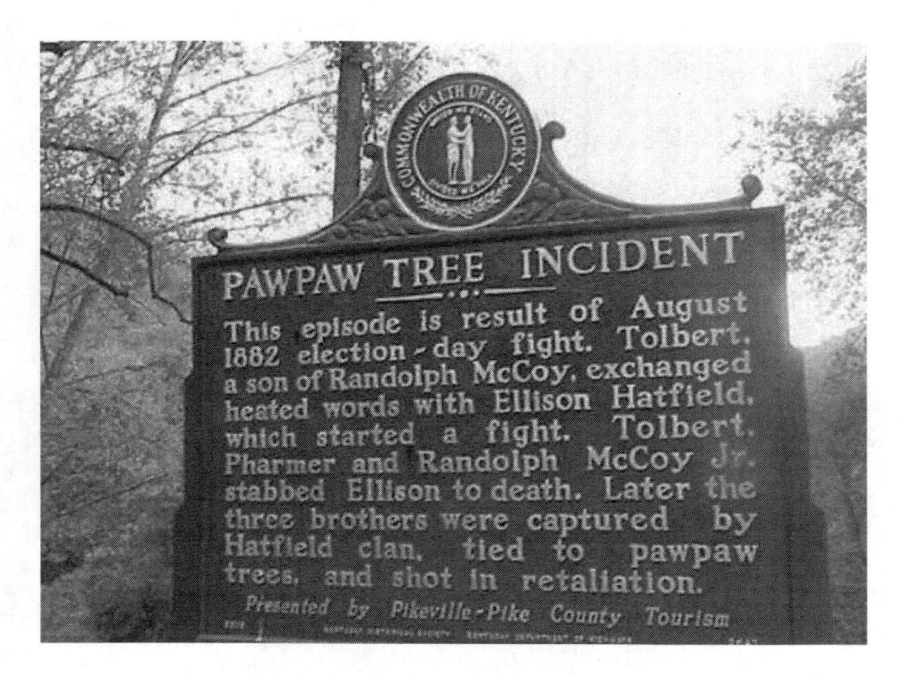

PAWPAW TREE INCIDENT

This episode is result of August 1882 election-day fight. Tolbert, a son of Randolph McCoy, exchanged heated words with Ellison Hatfield, which started a fight. Tolbert, Pharmer and Randolph McCoy Jr. stabbed Ellison to death. Later the three brothers were captured by Hatfield clan, tied to pawpaw trees, and shot in retaliation.

Presented by Pikeville-Pike County Tourism

Coordinates: 37° 37.098' N, 82° 9.933' W.

Marker is in McCarr, Kentucky, in Pike County.

Execution, Assassination, Bushwhacked - call it what you will but the word that probably describes what happened that day just on the Kentucky side of the Tug River was nothing short of Cowardly Murder. When they arrived on the Kentucky side of the River, there were some Paw Paw trees just up the river bank a little ways. Devil Anse told Johnse and Cap to tie the McCoy boys to the three trees that were closest together.

One story goes:

Tolbert the oldest McCoy tried to explain to Devil Anse once again about what had taken place during the fight. It was pretty evident and self-explanatory just by looking at the huge gash still open and leaking blood and pus down one side of Tolbert's head. Devil Anse didn't want to hear Tolbert's excuses; or that he was only protecting himself. He criticized Tolbert for his ambiguous statements. Devil Anse wasn't even there when the fight took place, but he knew what had happened. Remember this is Devil Anse, he knew everything and could do anything. Now he's getting ready to take extravagant measures to show everyone just how mean he really was.

Devil Anse told his guys to dismount; at least twenty – three in number, most of these men were the same ones that were in his gang of Wildcats. You could see the rancor and malice in Devil Anse's eyes as he told them to strip down butt-necked. That was just another way to show his power and remove whatever dignity the boys may have had left. He told them, you came into this world naked you can go out the same way.

Devil Anse then told his men tie the three boys to the trees. Then he directed each man as to whom he wanted them to kill and upon finishing said, "Fire!" The shots rang out. The spite and hatred were as relevant on his face as the paw paw leaves that floated to the ground with every shot and shake of the trees. It sounded like a small war. All the men fired an exorbitant amount of bullets into the McCoys. Finally, when the smoke cleared there was Tolbert and Pharmer slumped over just riddled with bullets. Crazy Jim

Vance said, "Those boys are bleeding like a stuck pig," laughing as if it were funny. He was giving reference to the pig again. Then everyone's attention turned to the third McCoy, just a teenage boy it was Randall Jr. or "Bud" as most knew him. He was next to the youngest son of Randall and Sarah McCoy. He was still standing, with not a mark on him. It was the way Devil Anse had it planned.

He had told everyone whom to shoot and no one was given Randall Jr's name, he was still among the living. Remember when the fight was taking place a couple of days earlier; Randall Jr. didn't really do anything other than try to separate Tolbert and Ellison. Everyone knew that the boy was innocent of any wrong doing.

Devil Anse walked over to Randall Jr. and said, "If you'll get on your knees and beg, I will let you live." Randall Jr. supposedly looked at his brothers then looked Devil Anse Hatfield right square in the eyes and said, "Too Hell with you Hatfields." Devil Anse turned to walk away then unprovoked quickly turned back around and shot the youngest boy of the three. Upon emptying his pistol into Randall Jr. he mounted up and rode off back towards West Virginia.

Cap Hatfield looked at the others and said, "Now boys that right there was <u>A Real McCoy</u>." Supposedly, that's where the old saying, "The Real McCoy' comes from.

Jim Vance walked over to each McCoy, knowing they were already dead, but as a symbolic message of "don't mess with the Hatfields," shot each in the head one last time and said "Dead men don't talk" Then he looked at every man who was there and said "If anyone of you sons of ****** ever tells that I was here I will hunt you down and kill you." What happened here today will go to the grave with each of us. Then he got on his horse and rode back across the Tug River to catch up to Devil Anse. That was the story told by some. Then, there was the story Cottontop told from the witnesses stand in a Pike County Courtroom at his murder trial. (another chapter)

    The question I always wondered about growing up was why Devil Anse had to do what the Pike County Courts would have done anyway? Instead of a firing squad, the Courts would have ordered a hanging but the result would have been the same. They would have still been dead (except for Randall Jr.) as he would have been found not guilty because he hadn't done anything wrong.

    The execution of the three McCoy boys was even worse than what they had done to Ellison. At least Ellison had a fighting chance, and his hands weren't tied to a tree when he was killed. Devil Anse was lower than Jim Vance's dog for doing this. He was no better than the McCoy boys, and he was dead sober. At least, Ellison Hatfield and Tolbert McCoy were drunk the day of the fight.

    When the McCoys came to retrieve the bodies of Randall and Sarah's three sons the only way to describe the scene was horrific. One of the witnesses said the mountains were untamed and ferocious "the banks of the Tug River was littered with three testaments to the savageness of the Hatfields". Devil Anse's barbaric and tendency for savagery was evident at the base of each tree where the McCoys' bullet riddled and mutilated bodies laid bound with their hands tied to each tree.

Since the Paw Paw is a fruit. The task of polarization is left to various species of flies and beetles. They were already on the scene when the three boys were killed it didn't take long for them to transform or metamorphosis into maggots and begin to devour the three caucuses."

Had a person known what we do now' someone could have told Randall "the worst is yet to come." He still had two more sons and two daughters he would lose before the feud was over. The old saying "No matter how bad a situation is it could always be worse." It could not have been truer. As bad as this day was, a fiery hell was coming, and Jim Vance and "Cap" Hatfield were bringing it.

The McCoy's were tied to three trees with the view of the Tug River in the background.
Please do not copy without the written permission of Fred McCoy

Roseanna and Johnse

Sleeping with the Enemy

Illustrated by Michael Hatter
Please do not copy these sketches without the written permission of Fred McCoy.

Thinking about Roseanna and Johnse, one cannot help but feel sorry for the two of them. They were in love, but everything seemed to go wrong. First, they were the off-spring of the two clan leaders of the most famous feud in America, if not the world. Secondly, no matter how hard they tried to make it work, it just seemed like the cards were stacked against them. At every turn there was a new obstacle blocking their path that kept them from being together.

Roseanna McCoy, daughter of Randall and Sarah McCoy was born on March 21, 1859 in Pike County, Kentucky. Roseanna was Randall's favorite child. She had black hair and beautiful eyes. As she got older, she became known as one of the most attractive girls in Pike County, Kentucky. She was a loving girl who believed that there was good in everyone- even a Hatfield.

Roseanna loved her poppy, and they were very close. In his eyes, she could do no wrong. She was his world, his little girl. However, that would soon change.

In 1878, at the Hog Trial of Floyd Hatfield, Roseanna first notices Johnson (Johnse) Hatfield. Then, on Election Day In the spring of 1880, Roseanna McCoy would meet up with Johnse again. Roseanna thought he was very handsome. Johnse and Roseanna's affinity for one another was mutual, and Johnse convinced Roseanna to leave the election grounds with him to go for a walk. Even though Roseanna knew Johnse's reputation for being a lover boy she went with him anyway.

It is said that Johnse gave Roseanna her first kiss that night. Some said it was love at first sight. Others said it was just lust. Who knows what Johnse thought? As for Roseanna, she only had eyes for Johnse. Some say it was a match made in heaven, if it were not for the "Devil."

It was getting late, and by the time they returned from their stroll in the woods, everyone was gone. Roseanna fearing her father's wrath for being late, and also wanting to spend more time with her new love, went home with Johnse where she stayed the night under a Hatfield roof. Devil Anse was outraged at Johnse for bringing a McCoy girl to his home. In the end, Anse finally agreed for her to stay the night with the condition that Johnse was to take her back across the Tug River to her home at the break of dawn and Johnse agreed. That night Johnse snuck into his sister's room where Roseanna was sleeping and told her he loved her and wanted to marry her. She was so happy.

The next day when she returned home, Randall, eventhough, he was happy to see his daughter, he was still upset that she had stayed away from home. She told her father that Johnse wanted to ask for her hand in marriage. Randall was hurt that Roseanna would even consider marriage to a Hatfield. How could she betray her family? Especially, after her uncle Asa Harmon had been murdered by a Hatfield or Crazy Jim Vance years earlier. He told her to leave and go live with the Hatfield's.

Roseanna was a one-man woman. She would risk the love of her family for the love of Johnse, not knowing it wouldn't last. Roseanna's brother took her to the Tug River where Johnse was waiting for her to return. When they returned, Devil Anse was furious with Johnse because he was told to leave her and not bring her back. It was said that Devil Anse "beat the fire" out of Johnse for disobeying his orders. However, Lavicey reluctantly agreed to let her stay for a while. Devil Anse told Johnse he "would never agree to let them marry."

The common understanding seems to have been that Johnse held her out, in the neighborhood, as his wife. Both West Virginia and Kentucky were what is known as, Common Law states. Under the common law, no civil authority or ceremony, and no religious ceremony were necessary to the creating of the status of husband and wife, which might be done by the mutual consent of the parties, and a public declaration of their intentions to become husband and wife.

Roseanna stayed there for a while, for how long we don't really know. Later, Lavicey told Roseanna that because she was a McCoy, it was time she returned to her family. Roseanna replied, "Are you asking me to leave?" to which Lavicey answered, "Yes, and this time don't come back."

We don't want to over-emphasize Johnse and Roseanna's relationship. Johnse was said to have been Rosanna's first and only love. However, Johnse was promiscuous with several other women. The relationship ended abruptly after she had already been impregnated by the son of the Devil.

Over the course of the relationship there would be killings on both sides that each family had to endure. At the peak of their relationship is when Roseanna became pregnant. So again Roseanna returned home, with her heart broken, to see if they would accept her back into the family. As Sarah and Roseanna we're talking, Roseanna informed her mother that she was with child. Sarah knew Randall would be very upset, and that he wouldn't let her return home.

In her third month of pregnancy Sarah sent Roseanna to live with her aunt Betty and Uncle Uriah (my great, great grandfather and grandmother), in Burnwell, Ky. Roseanna went willingly. She felt abandon like she been tossed away. Her father didn't want her, and Johnse couldn't be with her, because of his family.

She told her aunt Betty that no one wanted her, and that she had no place left to go. Roseanna stayed with her uncle Uriah and Aunt Betty and gave birth to a beautiful baby girl in 1881, whom she named her Sarah Elizabeth, Sarah after her mother and Elizabeth after Aunt Betty. Eight months later Sarah Elizabeth came down with the measles and died. This devastated Roseanna. Her life had not turned out the way she thought it would. She and her father were at odds. Her brothers were killed by the Hatfield's. The Hatfield's didn't want her, in fear of making the McCoy's even angrier. Eight years later in 1889 at the age of 29 Roseanna would pass away from pneumonia. (Not from a broken heart as all the romance novels have always suggested, simple pneumonia, which was pretty common back in those days.)

Little Sarah Elizabeth was buried on a mountain at Burnwell, Kentucky. The location is near Uriah and Betty McCoy's home place. (Uriah and Betty McCoy were my Great-Great-Grandparents). Roseanna would be buried at Dils Cemetery in Pikeville, Kentucky next to her father and mother. Some say that Randall never forgave Rosanna, yet out of sixteen children, she's the only one that is buried beside him. He always said she was his favorite, and I think that proved it. Devil Anse said that Johnse was so lazy that if he had a third hand, he would need an extra pocket to put it in. Johnse would later marry four other times and have six children. Johnse died in 1922 of a heart attack.

Sam McCoy kills Bill Staton

Self Defense not Revenge

Big Sam McCoy

Illustrated by Michael Hatter
Please do not copy these sketches without the written permission of Fred McCoy

Bill Staton was the sole witness at the famous Pig Trial. It was his lying testimony that catapulted the feud to the next level. Some have said he was drunk and clowning around at the trial, liquored up, showing off, and not taking it seriously because after all it was just a pig. Others have said he was afraid of losing his job and wanted to impress Devil Anse with his loyalties to the Hatfields. Even though Bill was a nephew of Ole Ran'l, he was a brother-in-law of Ellison Hatfield.

Bill lived on the West Virginia side of the Tug River and was in contact with the Hatfield's daily. He may have thought if he took up for Floyd Hatfield it would make it easier on him. After all, when this pig trial was over, he still had to go back across the Tug River and get along with the Hatfield's.

Who really knows what he was thinking or why Bill gave the testimony that he thought the pig belonged to Floyd Hatfield? After all he was a peculiar fellow to say the least. We will never know why he said what he did but no doubt it did change the outcome of the trial and was the very thing that Floyd Hatfield needed to get a not-guilty verdict.

Once Bill Staton took the stand and said he had seen Floyd Hatfield's mark on that pig it was all over. Five of the McCoy's had a different take on Bill's testimony. They knew Bill Staton and his reputation as a drunkard and liar. They were not about to take Bill Staton's word over Randall's.

The five McCoy's knew Randall was a man of his word, and they believed Randall McCoy's account that the pig was, in fact, his. The only McCoy that sided with the Hatfield's was Selkerk McCoy. The best way to describe, Selkerk was that he was so skinny he'd have to stand up twice just to make a shadow.

Selkirk shaking like a leaf in a wind storm in a stuttering and wispy voice said he was going to side with the Hatfield's. So the final count was seven to five in favor of Floyd Hatfield being not guilty. This was a major disappointment for Randall as he had always believed in the justice system. It was like having the wind knocked out of Ole Ran'l, a man who was known for doing the right thing. He would give you the shirt off his back but don't try to take it from him. He quietly left the court room. It' wasn't the pig. He just wanted justice and an apology. It was that simple.

However, neither would come that day. What did come after court had been dismissed was one of the McCoy's stopped Bill Staton outside and ask him to describe what Floyd Hatfield's pig marking (notch) had looked like? To which Bill replied in a drunken stutter, "How the hell would I know," when ask for details Bill declined to elaborate further he laughed and walked away.

As for Selkirk, he attempted to explain that he had a family to think about. "If I don't work they don't eat!" he said. Not only did Selkirk work for Devil Anse but so did Albert McCoy and L. D. McCoy, who were both related to Selkirk.

It was some two years later that "Squirrel Hunt'en Sam" or "Big Sam" McCoy as some called him and Paris McCoy, both nephews of Randall, would meet up with Bill Staton again. It was a fact in those parts of Eastern Kentucky that Big Sam was the best squirrel hunter around. Sam would rather squirrel hunt than to eat. That was his pastime and a way of putting food on the table at the same time. According to stories handed down, Sam and Paris McCoy were out squirrel hunting. It was early morning, and they were some

20 yards from one another. Each sitting under a hickory tree just waiting for the fog to clear and the squirrels to start stirring. It is not known if Bill Staton was on his way home from laying out all night or actually going hunting. What is known is that he happened upon Paris McCoy and got the drop on him. Paris was taking a leak, when he turned and saw Bill; however, it was too late to reach for his gun leaning up against the hickory tree. Bill said, "I got you now you son of a *****," and shot at Paris as he took a dive for cover. When suddenly through the fog and mist a voice said, "I got you, you lying *******" his response was bursting with hatred and fury, another shot rang out echoing through the woods. It was Big Sam McCoy. As Bill Staton was turning around Big Sam had shot him in the face. Big Sam then ran to check on Paris, who had only been wounded by the shot hitting him in the lower back. If he hadn't made a dive for cover, he would have surely been a dead man.

    Ellison Hatfield who had married Bill Staton's sister was upset over Bill being killed and was relentless in pressing charges against Paris and Sam. Warrants were issued by Ellison Hatfield's brother "Judge" Wall Hatfield for Paris and Big Sam. Their uncle Randall accompanied them to turn themselves into the Sheriff.

    When the trial came around, both Sam and Paris McCoy were found not guilty and Bill Stanton's death ruled self-defense. Sam, Paris, and the Randall McCoy family never forgave Ellison for the false and vengeful charges placed against them, even though they knew it was self-defense. Remember Bill Staton shot Paris in the back.

Cabin Massacre

It was a cold, bitter morning on Saturday, December, 31st 1887. Devil Anse, was quoted as saying, "all the McCoy's have to die" when talking to "Cap" his son, his uncle Jim Vance and some of his Wildcats. That way, the McCoys couldn't give any damaging evidence against them if they were arrested and transported to Pike County for trial. Remember, Randall and Sarah both had gone to Devil Anse's where he had their three boys locked up in an old school house. Sarah was even allowed inside to talk to her boys for the last time.

Had Devil Anse not made that mistake, there wouldn't have been any witnesses as to him saying he would "return them to Kentucky and that if Ellison died, then so would the three McCoy boys." This was damming evidence against him and his clan. Devil Anse had gathered some of his Logan Wildcats and informed them what they were about to do to Randall and his family.

Crazy Jim Vance and thirteen of Devil Anse's followers climbed onto their horses. As they were preparing to ride off one of the Wildcats, (thought to have been Alex Messer) ask Devil Anse aren't you coming with us? Devil Anse said, "no, I'm feeling a little under the weather" one of the Wildcats spoke up and said how about we put this off until tomorrow or even Monday, when you're feeling better?

Devil Anse said, "you men go ahead, and give'em hell." His uncle Jim Vance undertook Devil Anse's orders with pride and led the assassins towards Randall McCoy's home place to reap havoc. As they rode off Crazy Jim Vance yelled "I hereby declare war against the McCoys." They all laughed. Tom Chambers removed his pistol from its holster pointed it towards the sky and hollered out Yee Haw! As he fired his gun, they all laughed again and headed towards Kentucky.

After only a mile or so, away some of the men started discussing the fact that Devil Anse had this big plan to kill Randall McCoy and his family but said he wasn't feeling well enough to participate. Four of the men had a change of heart and said they thought they too would sit this one out. They said they were feeling a little under the weather themselves. Since the Devil, himself was not going, why should they? Crazy Jim was said to have gotten quarrelsome with the four men because they were changing their minds about going. In the end, the four rode off back towards their homes.

It is said this is where Jim Vance gave his famous speech that went something like "if anyone of you that goes forward from here on, gets there and backs out I will shoot you myself." It seems like the West Virginia Hatfield's were nocturnal as most of their pathetic and outlandish escapades took place at night under cover of darkness. Maybe they needed all the edge they could get. After all they were going up against an elderly man – an elderly woman - a kid still in school and a bunch of children. (This could be bad)

As the assassins approached the McCoy's cabin, they could see the smoke rising up and out of the chimney. It was one of the coldest nights they'd had all winter; it was also a full moon. Their intent was to tie the horses down the path always and walk up through the creek. However, they didn't count on Blue belly being home. Blue belly was Randall's old coon hound dog. He was half blue tick and half red bone. He was mostly red all over except his belly, and it was covered in blue specs so that's how he got his name. They got too close to the property. Now the dog is barking, and Blue belly only barked at two things. When he had a coon up a tree and when there was a stranger in close proximity to their property. Ol Ran'l had raised Blue belly from a pup and knew the difference in the dogs bark. This was no coon; someone was here.

Upon arriving at Randall's home Jim Vance and his clan surround the house. Cap Hatfield told Cottontop, "You're noisier than a fox in a chicken coup" as he gave him a rifle and positioned him behind a tree for cover. Crazy Jim Vance called to everyone in the cabin to come out. When they refused a shot was fired. Calvin returned fire, which was met with a shower of bullets relentlessly hitting their home.

Sarah told Randall to leave. Once the Hatfields knew that Randall had left they would leave everyone else alone. However, Randall refused saying " I don't think that would work, with crazy Jim Vance out there it's no telling what he'll do to you, and the children, I'm not leaving you." He took his shot gun and begins firing. Although Randall was out numbered he retained a sense of composer and remained calm. Since crazy Jim was not getting the surrender he wanted he decided to set fire to the house. He ran up to the house where he saw cotton hanging, grabbed it and setting it on fire placed it near the door.

Tom Chambers ran to the side of the house where there were some pine branches lying on the ground and picked one up attaching cotton to it making a small torch, he set it afire. Then he climbed upon the roof and tried to remove a board in order to drop his flaming branch into the loft. Before Chambers could drop the torch Randall had shot through the roof hitting him in the hand. This caused him to drop his burning branch and lose his hand, including all of his fingers. Not being able to withstand the pain to his hand Tom Chambers fell off the roof screaming in agony. He ran crying back towards Jim Vance's location for cover. Screaming all the way "the Ol man shot me."

As the flames and smoke began to fill the house, Calvin yelled for his sisters to try to put out the fire. Alifair, Fanny, Josephine, and Adelaide grabbed what milk they had in the house to attempt to douse the flames. Alifair who was stricken with polio, said she would go get water from the well. "They won't shoot me" she told the others. She couldn't have been more wrong as she opened the door with water pail in hand and limped towards the well she was heard screaming, "Cap" as if she saw him and to let him know it was her. It would be the last word she ever spoke. Just then a blast rang out, and bullets struck Alifair, and she fell to the ground. The fire was still burning so they used some butter that they had in a churn sitting in the corner, but the flames kept growing. By then the house was filled with thick black smoke.

Calvin told Randall that he would try to distract them by going out the front door, and heading towards the corn crib. Before Randall could stop him, he was gone. Randall hearing the children gasping for air realizes the cabin is fully engulfed in flames, and the situation is even more treacherous then he realized. He had been so busy shooting back he had gotten tunnel vision and hadn't noticed what was going on around him. He sends the children out of the back door to hide in the woods. Calvin is shot down within five feet of the front door, and was fatally wounded.

Sarah saw her daughter get shot and went out the door towards where Alifair's body was laying. Crazy Jim Vance said, "we're here to kill all you sons of ******" Crazy Jim then took the butt of his gun and vigorously beat Sarah in the head until she collapsed face down on the ground then he along with Johnse Hatfield began kicking Sarah. The way they abused the elderly woman was unconscionable.

Crazy Jim thought she was dead. He shouted to Cap, "She's flopping like a chicken with its head cut off." Let's get the Hell out of here. By then the night sky was lit up from the fire. You could hear Randall and Sarah's neighbors coming to the rescue to see if they could help. As Randall exits the burning cabin after ensuring the younger children were safe from the fire. He sees Sarah and his two children motionless on the ground and fires both barrels at the Assassins as their riding off back towards West Virginia. It is believed that this is when he shot Johnse, wounding him.

When the neighbors arrived, they saw that Calvin and Alifair had been murdered. Randall saw Sarah lying motionless on the ground with everyone gathering around her. He just knew she was dead as well. He ran over to where Sarah was he called her name "Sarah!" She made a faint groaning sound. She was alive, at least for now.

Sarah had been beaten so brutally that she suffered a broken arm and hip not to mention her head had been crushed. She had lost so much blood that by the time help came her hair was frozen to the cold ground.

At the end of the ambush, Randall had lost two more children. His wife was savagely beaten, and their home was burned to the ground. Their son Jim McCoy only lived about a mile away. So they took Sarah there. Randall buried two more of their children. Calvin and Alifair were laid to rest at the same cemetery as Tolbert, Randall Jr. and Phamer. Roseanna returned home and helped take care of her mother.

It was said that Sarah had to use a cane to help her get around the rest of her life. This was due to the injuries she received from Crazy Jim Vance on the night of the New Year's Massacre. Sarah died in 1894 after the feud trials had come to an end.

Confessions of Charley Gillespie

Charles S. Howell wrote many reports on the Hatfields and McCoys and their "war of extermination" as he called it. We will be critiquing many of his reports. Mr. Howell was one of the few who called it like he saw it. The old saying "The buck stops here" could not have been truer. He didn't play favorites. He wrote it like it was. Mr. Howell's slogan was let the chips fall where they may. Mr. Howell obtained a written confession from Charley Gillespie. One of the Hatfields hench man who accompanied them on the New Year's Massacre. One newspaper called it "a thrilling recital of Bloody Deeds."

Within a month of killing Randall's daughter and son, along with beating his wife and burning the cabin down Cap and Johnse Hatfield were on the lame. They eluded to the West.

They along with Old Jim Vance were prominent figures during the massacre. They were in fear of not only the McCoys seeking revenge for their deadly deeds, but everyone in both West Virginia and Kentucky was upset with what they had done to the two children and Sarah McCoy.

Barely nineteen years old, Charley Gillespie stated he had been swindled into going along on the midnight ride by Cap Hatfield, who had told him they were going to have some "fun."

Charley went along with Cap and the others instead of fun, he found that he was now an accessory to two murders and arson by burning the McCoy's house down under the most revolting circumstances. Approximately, ten months after the Massacre, Detectives found Charley Gillespie and arrested him. **Below is his complete and actual statement word-for-word as he told it along with all the chilling details of that night.**

"On the first day of last January I was at home, when Cap. Hatfield came along and said: "Charley, we are going over into Kentucky tonight to have some fun." Get a horse and meet us and go along. Well, I did not know what was up, but I told Cap, I would be on hand, after a little trouble, I got a horse and was at the rendezvous, where I found Cap, Johns, Ellis, Bob and Ellison Hatfield, Old Jim Vance, Ellison Mounts, and a man who goes by the name of both Mitchell and Chambers, whom I know by the name of 'guerrilla.'

Jim Vance was in command of the party, and it was agreed at the start, before the real object of the trip was disclosed, that all should yield to everything he said and to do all that he might order us to do. It has been claimed that the whole Hatfield neighborhood was with us that night. This is not true. There were nine of us, and the nine I have mentioned.

"Arriving at a convenient distance from the McCoy house I was first made acquainted with the real object of our trip. Vance told us that if old Randall McCoy, and his son 'Cal' were out of the road, every material witness against the men who had taken part in the murder of the three McCoy boys would be removed, and there could be no conviction of any of them, even if they at some time might be arrested for it. All had become tired of dodging the officers of the law, and wished to be able to sleep at home beside better bed fellows than Winchester rifles, and occasionally take off their boots when they went to bed. This was the reason that 'Old Jim' Vance gave us, Cap and Johns Hatfield agreed with him.
"We determined if the family did not come out when we should warn them to, to shoot through the windows and door of the house from the ends and sides with our Winchesters, volley after volley, until all inside would be dead or disabled. The only reply the McCoys made to our demand to come out was to bar and barricade the doors and prepare to fight us till the last. We shot through the windows and doors, and our shooting was responded to by 'Old Ran'l' and 'Cal,' the former with a double-barreled shot gun and the other with a

Winchester. We had to be very careful, as both were good shots.

"I must tell you right here that I was not one of those who were doing the shooting. Me and one of the other Hatfields was put out along the road to act as guards, to see that no one came up, or that no one got past us. We never went near the house until the house was burning, and all was on their way back to Hatfield's house. When they came up Ellison Mounts said to me: 'Well, we killed the boy and girl, and I am sorry of it. We have made a bad job of it. We didn't get the man we wanted at all (meaning 'old Ran'l). If we had got him; it would have been all right, and our work would not have been lost. There will be trouble over this.' I asked him about the fight as we went along home, and he told me how Chambers had crawled upon the roof to get at those inside and to fire the house, when 'Ran'l McCoy heard him, and firing at him through the shingles, shot his hand off behind the knuckles. He said Chambers got down, tied his hurt hand, and taking his Winchester, began shooting again. It took some time to get the McCoys out, but finally, the door opened and 'Cal.' Ran out at the top of his speed toward a corn crib. Several banged away at him, but none of the shots took effect, and one or two more shots were fired, when he was seen to jump up and fall forward. We went to him and found him dead, with a big hole in the back of his head. The girl came out of one of the two dwelling houses and wanted to get into the one where the family was, as some of the men told her to go back, but she knew them and named them, and she was killed. 'Cap' was blamed for this, but I think Mounts did it. I could not find out who struck old Mrs. McCoy with the butt of the revolver, but I think Mounts did this, too. The hammer of the revolver penetrated her skull, and when she fell several of the men jumped upon her, breaking her ribs, and when they left her thought she was dead.

"I had let my horse go on the way to the house of the McCoys, and had to get up behind Mounts, better known as 'Cotton-Top' and 'Cotton-Eye,' because he has white hair and white eyes. On the way, home he talked a great deal. Once he said, 'If John Hatfield had not shot before we were ready, there would not have been one of the McCoys in that house alive now. That shot gave them inside a correct idea of the location of some of the men, and they kept us well in sight right along thereafter. They kept us so far away that it was a long time before we got up to the house, and unable to do anything. (End of Statement).

Courtesy of: West Virginia Archives and History
http://www.wvculture.org/history/hatfieldmccoyarticles.html

The above statement was taken by Detective P.A. Campbell and sworn to by Gillespie before the Mayor of Wellston. He was then incarcerated and taken to jail. Where he was visited by J. Lee Ferguson, Prosecuting Attorney of Pike County, Kentucky, and to him, the story was retold. After that Charley, Gillespie was taken to the jail at Pike County Kentucky by James (Jim) McCoy son of Randall McCoy.

Confession of Ellison Hatfield.

"Better to remain silent and to be thought of as a fool. Then to speak and remove all doubt".

Confession and statement of Ellison Hatfield word-for-word as he told it.

Pike County, Oct. 29. 1888 – This is my true and honest statement concerning the Hatfield-McCoy trouble which I propose to make at any and all times: *"In 1882 Wall Hatfield, who was a Justice of the Peace in Logan County, West Va., organized a band and administered an iron-clad oath to each. Alex Messer, 'Anse,' 'Capt.' And Johns Hatfield, Chas. Carpenter, myself and many others whose names I cannot tell at present, took three of the McCoy boys across Tug River. Charley Carpenter tied them to bushes, when 'Capt,' Johns, Anse and some of the others fired on them. Anse Hatfield shot Tolbert McCoy with a rifle and with a revolver. Alex Messer killed Randolph McCoy, a boy of thirteen years. Elias Hatfield opposed the killing of the boys; I did not aid the Hatfield gang in any way further, until New Year's night 1888, when nine of us, viz: James Vance, Sr., Cap. Johns, Bob and Black, Elliott Hatfield, Chas. Gillespie, French Ellis, Thos Mitchell alias Chambers, and myself went from Cap. Hatfield's house in Logan County, W. Va., to Randal McCoy's house in Pike County, Ky., and attacked the inmates by firing through the door. Old Jim Vance fired the house with lighted matches put in under the roof near the loft; about then I moved my position to the chimney end of the kitchen, in company with French Ellis; Cap and Elliott Hatfield fired into the loft at noises supposed to be made by Calvin McCoy. The girls, who slept in the kitchen, got up and said they were going to put out the fire. Jim Vance, Cap and Johns Hatfield ordered me to kill them if they showed themselves. Presently*
Miss Alfaria McCoy peered, being dressed in black. She begged Cap Hatfield to spare her life. I then shot her with a Winchester rifle, the ball passing through her body, she falling in a lifeless condition on the floor. Her sister Addie asked her if she were killed; her only answer was one word, 'Yes,' which

was the only word uttered by her after being shot. Addie remarked, 'farewell, sister, I hope to meet you beyond the grave.' Presently I got shot from the loft above. My arm being broken, I changed my position and quit fighting. About this time, Johns Hatfield knocked Mrs. Randall McCoy down and kicked her until life seemed extinct. Tom Mitchel alias Chambers, got three fingers shot off and a lot of bird shots in his body. Johns Hatfield was shot in the shoulder. The fire drove Calvin McCoy out of the house, and he was killed, both Cap and Johns Hatfield claiming, in a braggadocio manner that he did it. The fight lasted about an hour and a half, and when the house was in flames all over, we left, going through the mountains to Peter Creek, thence across the river into West Virginia. I fainted once from the loss of blood, so the crowd left me next morning at Jake Ferrell's, on Pigeon Creek. I managed to get to Harvy Duty's where I remained overnight and then went to my home, Sand Lick Creek, on Guyandotte River where Dr. Will Brown dressed my wounds. Dr. Hudgiss of Logan C. H., dressed Tom Mitchell's hand.

I was led into this scrape by the older Hatfields and have seen no peace since I killed the McCoy girl.

The Hatfields made me work all day and then aid them in meanness at night. The Winchester with which I killed Alfaria McCoy, I gave to Dan Cunningham for his kindness to me since my arrest – signed Ellison Hatfield. Witness T. M. Gibson, D. W. Cunningham, Mary M. Daniels, Jane Blackburn and Margaret Blackburn.

Ellison Hatfield was the son of the Ellison Hatfield, who was stabbed and shot on the Election grounds at Blackberry Kentucky. He was also the grandson of Devil Anse Hatfield.

Courtesy of: West Virginia Archives and History
http://www.wvculture.org/history/hatfieldmccoyarticles.html

Battle of Grapevine

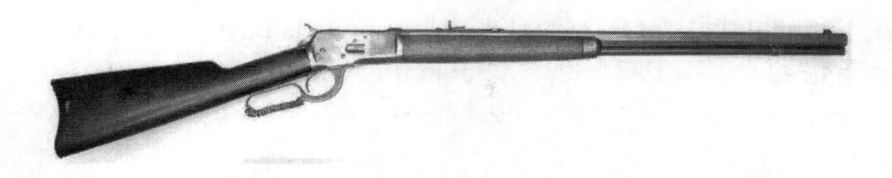

Attitudes and public perception changed after the Hatfield's failed in their attempt to "Kill all the McCoys." During the New Year's Eve attack on Randall's cabin two more of his kids were killed. Those who had personally witnessed the aftermath saw the victims as they lay frozen to the ground from the blood that had spilled out of their bodies. They couldn't have been any more traumatized. The two children, Alifair and Calvin had been sleeping in their beds when the murderers arrived. Now they were outside their home still dressed in their long johns and night gown riddled with bullets. Both with their eyes still open wide, meaning they died instantly. They were more than likely looking right at the killer as the trigger was being squeezed. Over to the side was Mrs. McCoy, Randall's wife and the deceased children's mother, barely alive and beaten so bad she was unrecognizable.

How could she have survived such a brutal attack? She too was frozen to the ground by the blood on her head and in her hair as well as coming out of her mouth and nose.

It was reported that they literally had to pry her from the ground leaving some skin, hair, and brains behind.

When Bad Frank Phillips walked around looking at the aftermath of what the Hatfields and Crazy, Jim Vance had done he thought to himself how can anyone have this much hatred towards a family? What in the hell is wrong with those Hatfields?

Frank said in a stunned, grieving voice, "There are no rules from this day forth." After seeing Alifair's body he said, "We are going to seek retribution for the senseless killings of these children and for the beating of that sweet, old woman, Mrs. McCoy. Not a Hatfield involved with what took place here in this cowardly attack is safe from this day forth. Any man with a weak stomach or of weak mind, need not accompany me in the apprehension of these bushwhackers. It's not going to be pleasant when I catch up to them."

Frank Phillips seemed to be on a mission after the "Cabin Massacre." He said, "Kentucky and West Virginia Mountains and rivers will flow with Hatfield's blood until there is justice for all the McCoy killings that have taken place." Frank got word that the Hatfield's would be crossing at Grapevine later in the day. They were in fear of retaliation from their attack, killings, and burning of the home of Randall McCoy. They were heading back up into the mountains once again to hide out.

The story had gone out across the wire and was already running in newspapers in New York. People all over the country were in shock that the feud had gone on so long. They were wondering how Randall McCoy had lost so many of his children to these murderous Hatfields. They were asking why? Why hasn't someone stepped in and put a stop to this feud?

Frank and his posse headed towards Grapevine, and Jim McCoy said, "If the good lord willing and the creeks don't rise; we'll be there by noon." Grapevine is located near Matewan; WV. Frank led the charge, and the two sides fought tooth and nail in what become known as the Battle at Grapevine Creek.

Eventually, Johnse Hatfield, Cap Hatfield, Ellison (Hatfield) Mounts and several others were arrested for the cabin massacre as well as the execution of the three boys.

JUSTICE OR NOT?

Indicted in Pike County for the execution of the three McCoy boys was Devil Anse Hatfield. Others were Johnson "Johnse" Hatfield, William "Cap" Hatfield, Elias Hatfield, Wall Hatfield, Sam Mahon, Dock Mayhorn, Plyant, Mayhorn, John Whitt, Tom Chambers, Charley Carpenter, Lark Varney, Andy Varney, Alex Messer, Selkerk McCoy, L.D. McCoy, Dan Whitt, and Ellison (Cottontop Mounts) Hatfield.

Indicting them for their crimes was one thing, getting them arrested and brought back to Kentucky was another. At the trial and according to Cottontop (Mounts) Hatfield, he said, "they took the three McCoy boys back across the water, and they tied them to trees, and Devil Anse told them they could pray, but before they could get through praying Johnse had done went and shot Pharmer in the head." Cottontop said Uncle Devil Anse shot Tolbert, and Alex Messer shot Bud (Randall Jr.) Every one of these men who were indicted was brought to Justice or at least appeared in court and sentenced. (EXCEPT) the Ring Leader, the one known as Devil Anse Hatfield.

Devil Anse allowed his brother's son to be hung by the neck on the Court House square. He allowed his sons to be sentence to life in prison, his brother to die in prison and his uncle Jim Vance to be killed. However, he hid out, focusing on no one except himself. This doesn't sound like a leader and mentor whom some people would have you believe he was. This sounds more like a man who would instigate problems then send his relatives, friends and employees to execute his plans that usually led to mayhem, while he stayed at home safe, (sick of course).

Don't look at this book from a Hatfield or McCoy perspective. Look at it objectively and in all fairness. Read the stories, better yet research the history of the feud yourself and see if the stories that have been told all our lives are true. Or were they perpetrated by one man. That man being Devil Anse Hatfield himself.

Perhaps it started out as a fluke; maybe Devil Anse just got caught up in the heat of the moment. With Randall McCoy completely refusing to talk to the media all they had left was Devil Anse. No doubt it made him feel superior each time he read the last story he gave in print. He liked the attention even more. He was known as an exhibitionist.

Over the years since the feud, a lot of people have joked instead of the posse chasing with guns, maybe they should have shown up with a camera. It seems like if there was a camera around Devil Anse would drop whatever he was doing gather his children together, give them all guns and pose for pictures.

    Let me reiterate Devil Anse was telling the newspaper one thing while he or his gang was doing something else to the McCoy's. Devil Anse was indicted for the kidnapping and murdering of the three McCoy boys. Devil Anse was never arrested nor returned to Kentucky to answer to the kidnapping and murder charges.

Devil Anse's Scapegoat

Ellison (Cottontop Mounts) Hatfield

Illustrated by Michael Hatter
Please do not copy these sketches without the written permission of Fred McCoy.

Over the years Cottontop has been referred to as a lot of things but, mostly he's been known as Devil Anse's scapegoat. It was thought that Devil Anse figured if the Kentucky Courts got to hang someone from West Virginia for the atrocities that had taken place in Kentucky against the McCoys, then maybe Deputy Sheriffs Frank Phillips and Jim McCoy would lighten up on attempting to bring him in to face his charges. When it came time for the hanging of Cottontop, Devil Anse stood fast.

Of course, Sarah McCoy and her daughter had already testified in court that it was, in fact, Cap Hatfield that had murdered Alifair on the night of the New Year's Massacre. Even Cottontop stated while on trial and right before he was hung, "The Hatfield's made him do it." It was always questioned what did Cottontop mean? The Hatfields made him kill Alifair or the Hatfields made him take the blame even when, Cap Hatfield had in fact pulled the trigger. I guess there are only two people who knew the truth to that question. That was Cap and Cottontop themselves. It seems there was nothing Devil Anse wouldn't do to keep himself out of jail. Why would "Cap" be any different?

With Cottontop's rudimentary skills with a rifle, it was dangerous for him to just have one in his possession much less tell him it's ok to shoot someone. It's a dang wonder, he didn't shoot some of their own men, like deadeye "Cap" Hatfield had done years earlier. Can you just picture Crazy Jim Vance and that gang? What a cluster that must have been. An equally good example would probably be the keystone cops. But this is what they ended up with after Devil Anse wormed his way out of not going. "Did I say that out loud?" I meant "got sick again."

It left the Logan Wildcats shorthanded so they had to give Cottontop a gun as well. After all there were only nine of them. They had their hands full remember you had old man Randall, who was now about sixty-three years old and his teenage son Calvin and oh almost forgot Randall's sixty-two year- old wife and four girls two of which were physically handicapped. Even though it has always been said the hanging of Cottontop was the last chapter in the feud and brought closure to the fighting families, I still think it was the killing of Jim Vance that seemed to open Devil Anse eyes. It made him realize he wasn't immune to being killed or brought to justice.

    The West Virginia Hatfield's were notorious for their bulling ways and barbaric lifestyle. If they were not fighting with someone else, then they were fighting with one another. It was common knowledge that Devil Anse had beaten the crap out of Johnse many times but like a domestic fight between a husband and wife, Johnse would always come back home and apologize to the "big man known as Devil." Even when he had done nothing to provoke the Devil, but that was Devil Anse Hatfield and his domain. While waiting to be hung Cottontop said he knew Jim Vance karkfumd him, and would come get him.

Illustrated by Michael Hatter
Please do not copy these sketches without the written permission of Fred McCoy.

Last Hanging Ever in Pike County

"Last Legal Hanging"

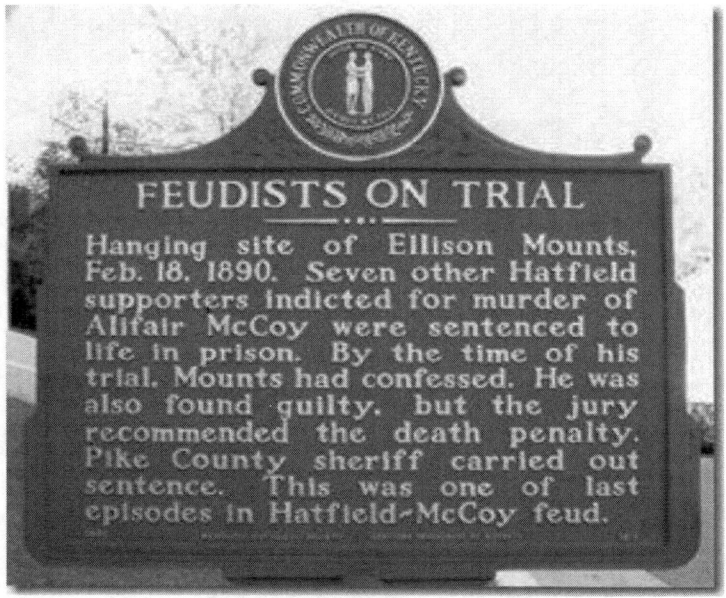

> **FEUDISTS ON TRIAL**
>
> Hanging site of Ellison Mounts, Feb. 18, 1890. Seven other Hatfield supporters indicted for murder of Alifair McCoy were sentenced to life in prison. By the time of his trial, Mounts had confessed. He was also found guilty, but the jury recommended the death penalty. Pike County sheriff carried out sentence. This was one of last episodes in Hatfield-McCoy feud.

Coordinates: 37 28.770 N 82 31.285 W

The execution of Ellison "Cottontop" Hatfield (Mounts) was on Feb 18th, 1890 in Pikeville, Kentucky for the murder of Alifair McCoy. She was shot on Dec 31st 1887 during the New Year's Eve Massacre.

The hanging drew a huge crowd of spectators. It was reported that the streets were clogged by wagon loads of men, women, and children. It was also reported that there was between 5,000 and 7,000 people that had come to Pikeville to witness the hanging and show support to Randall McCoy and his family. Devil Anse did not appear at the execution. The Sheriff pulled the lever that dropped the door and Cottontop to his death.

Everyone thought Devil Anse would ride into town to save Cottontop but once again, he seemed to "desert" the cause. It seems like when the odds were even or there were no women to beat up, or no children to execute, the Devil just wasn't interested. Even Devil Anse's own men wanted him to lead them to Pike County to rescue Cottontop, but it wasn't going to happen. Some got mad and said Devil Anse allowed Cotton to be sacrificed.

Randall McCoy attempted to stop the hanging, pleading with them not to hang a mentally challenged boy. People admired Randall even more saying how Cotton had killed Alifair, Randall's daughter, yet he was trying to spare Cotton's life. Randall wanted him to go to jail but not be hung. Randall told Cotton on the day of the hanging that he had already forgiven him for what he had done to his daughter.

Now Cotton needed to ask for God's forgiveness. He was buried in the prison cemetery. People dressed in their Sunday best and brought picnic lunches. They came from miles around to the view the hanging of Cottontop Mounts.

"Cottontop" (Mounts) Hatfield got his name from Daniel Mounts, who was his mother's husband. However, "Cottontop" was supposed to have been the product of an affair his mother Harriet had with her cousin Ellison Hatfield. Cottontop's mother died of a heart attack on her way to her son's hanging in 1890. The last words he ever spoke before they dropped the trap door was "the Hatfield's made me do it."

Cannot confirm but it was always thought that the man and woman on the bottom right of this picture is Randall and Sarah McCoy witnessing the hanging in 1890 of Ellison "Cottontop" (Hatfield) Mounts. After the beating in 1888 Sarah always wore a hat or bonnet when she was out in public due to her head injury and disfigurement.

Randall McCoy

Illustrated by Michael Hatter
Please do not copy these sketches without the written permission of Fred McCoy.

Patriarch, of the McCoy clan, was the fourth child of thirteen. Randall McCoy was born October 30, 1825 and died March 28, 1914. Randall lived on the Kentucky side of the Tug River.

He was a tall broad-shouldered man who wore a half-beard. After he returned from the war, he was always a serious man. By the end of the feud with Devil Anse Hatfield, he lost five children to the Hatfield's by execution, assassination, and fire.

Randall also lost his younger brother and nephew to assassination by the Hatfield's. Roseanna had died, and his granddaughter had passed away along with another son William McCoy.

After Randall married Sarah, they had sixteen children together. The family owned 300 acres of land in Pike County, Kentucky. Which was a fair amount of property for just farming. Randall McCoy and Devil Anse Hatfield's first conflict began when the Logan Wildcats (a group of deserters and renegades) assassinated Randall McCoy's brother Asa Harman McCoy in 1865.

Asa fought for the Union and was discharged and returned home to heal. He was not a threat to anyone. Even so, since he had, in fact, fought on the side of the North, Devil Anse's gang thought it would be ok to rid society of him. This was the first revenge killing of the feud, revenge for Asa Harmon having served with the Union Army.

Then in 1878, Floyd Hatfield was found to be in possession of one of Randall's pigs. In 1882, three of Randall's boys including his son and name sake Randall Jr. was killed. The boys were tied to Paw-Paw trees and executed by the Hatfield's in revenge for the death of Ellison Hatfield, Devil Anse's brother.

Randall was almost killed in 1888, when the Hatfield's set his cabin on fire and killed his daughter Alifair and son Calvin. They beat his wife so badly they thought she was dead. Randall was a hunter, a farmer, and a great provider for his family.

During the Civil war, considered a hero by his men and was held as a P.O.W. until the war ended in 1865. Randall was scarred for life as a result of being a P.O.W. and back then there wasn't anything called The Geneva Conventions Treaty. No doubt Randall McCoy was treated inhumanly as a P.O.W.

Some say Randall died an unhappy man. If someone had murdered eight members of your family and five of those eight were your children, they beat your wife and left her for dead, and after all that the ring leader behind it all was never brought to justice, would you be happy?

Randall was always considered by those who knew him as a Godly man. He was compared to Job in the Bible after losing his most valuable and prized possessions (his children). Even though he got frustrated many times with the justice system, he was persistent in pursuing justice for his children.

Over the years, some thought Randall had become withdrawn, but he retained a sense of equanimity. If people didn't believe Randall had been treated unfairly and was not a good man he would not have had so many of his friends and neighbors want to seek revenge on Devil Anse. These people "didn't have a dog in the fight" yet they came to Randall's defense. They put their lives in harm's way in order to take sides with Randall McCoy. That speaks volumes for the kind of integrity and values the man had.

When Randall did want to retaliate, Sarah would plead with him not to, and he would always agree with her in the end. Randall often agonized over his children and the outcome of his and Devil Anse's one-time friendship. Some said Randall never tried to make friends again with Devil Anse. Are you serious? He murdered five of Randall's children, and he's supposed to shake hands and make up. With friends like Devil Anse, Randall didn't need any enemies. Randall was a man beyond reproach.

After Jim Vance, was killed Devil Anse became reclusive in daily life. He was like a hermit he hid in different caves each night. If you're familiar with that area, there are plenty of caves. He was always on the move. When I was a kid, I would hear some of the older people talking, and they would laugh about how their dad or granddad would see one of the West Virginia Hatfield's and just funnin around would say who was that bunch of men riding towards Mate Creek earlier today. The Hatfield would say I don't know I haven't seen anybody, and the Hatfield would take back down the road towards Mate Creek what is now Matewan.

They talked about how they knew when the Hatfield got back to West Virginia and got word to Devil Anse, he would be skedaddling back up into the mountains when, in fact they hadn't even been anyone looking for him.

Randall died at the age of 88, in a house fire years after the feud had ended. The cause of the fire was never ruled on officially. Some thought he caught himself on fire, others speculated it had the Hatfield's M.O. (or Modus Operandi). Maybe they had beaten him like they did Sarah then left him for dead and set the house on fire once again.

There are some who said he's 88, and he's had a long life, let sleeping dogs lie, and call it an accident. Why add fuel to the fire and start the feud up again? On the death certificate it says, "died as a result of fire."

William Anderson Hatfield (AKA) Devil Anse

Illustrated by Michael Hatter please do not copy these sketches without the written permission of Fred McCoy.

Devil Anse Hatfield was born on September 9, 1839 and died January 6, 1921. He was born in Logan County, West Virginia. As of the printing of this book According to Google (BIO True Story) Devil Anse's occupation is listed as Murderer.

QUICK FACTS
- NAME: William Anderson Hatfield
- OCCUPATION: Murderer
- BIRTH DATE: September, 1839
- DEATH DATE: January, 1921
- PLACE OF BIRTH: Logan County, West Virginia
- PLACE OF DEATH: Logan County, West Virginia
- Nickname: Devil Anse

If one word had to describe Devil Anse (other than murderer) it would probably be a hedonist, he loved self-gratification. Life Magazine did a story on the Hatfield and McCoy feud in their May 22, 1944 issue. Life reported that "Devil Anse" Hatfield ordered the $3,000 marble statue of himself carved in Italy, and had it hauled up the mountainside by mules."

Devil Anse Hatfield was the leader of the Hatfield Clan on the West Virginia side of the Tug River. He also served in the Confederate Army exactly how long is not known. However, it is known that he did not complete his enlistment. Many of Devil Anse's relatives and sympathizers say he simply left early. To others, he was a deserter (when you leave the military prior to serving your commitment it is desertion.)

Devil Anse had several sons none was anymore notorious then Cap and Johnse Hatfield. Devil Anse and the West Virginia Hatfields practically ruled Logan County. The family had a reputation of been over bearing as well as bulling other people. Devil Anse's nickname was supposedly given to him as a young child when he was always getting into mischief and misbehaving. It was said that when Anse was about six years old his mother, Nancy Hatfield said, "Anse you're meaner than the Devil himself," and the name stuck. From then on his brothers and sisters started calling him Devil

Anse. Of course as the feud progressed, either Devil Anse or the news reporters figured it would enlighten the story if his nickname came in a more dramatic manner. Thence was born the story of Devil Anse defends off an entire Union Company all by himself and earns his nickname.

Devil Anse Hatfield and his wife Levicey had thirteen children between them. After Devil Anse left the Army, he formed the Logan Wildcats. A gang that was said to be one of the most feared guerrilla bands in the Tug River Valley area. They were feared because they were capable of anything. What started out as a good thing in protecting the home front quickly turned bad because of morals' or better yet the lack of morals? When this band of guerrillas got together they often forgot what they were there for and instead of protecting the home front, often it turned into tormenting the home front.

The gang often engaged in robbing and pillaging, while using the name of the Logan Wildcats as the justification for their actions. Their leader, Devil Anse, had total contempt for the law, before, during and after the feud.

Devil Anse and his cult following were responsible for the first death of the feud, Asa Harmon McCoy, Some have said Devil Anse and his Wildcats where responsible for "drawing first blood." Devil Anse and his family had a reputation that they were the supreme rulers of Logan County, West Virginia respecting neither man nor the law.

After the murder of the three McCoy boys, Devil Anse's son "Cap" assassinated Jeffery McCoy, the son of Asa Harmon McCoy. Jeffery was also Randall's nephew.

Devil Anse having personally executed the three McCoys was so vicious that everyone who knew him feared him. No one would attempt to rebuke anything Devil Anse ever said. It didn't matter if it was true or not, think of any bad or derogatory name you could call someone and the Devil was that and more. Devil Anse was indicted for the murders and crimes committed in Kentucky.

Devil Anse would live out his life in West Virginia never entering into Kentucky again in fear of being arrested and being hung for his crimes. Years after the fighting had stopped it was said that Devil Anse had offered to compensate the McCoys for their losses by giving them $20,000 if they agreed to drop the charges and indictments against him. Deputy Sheriff Jim McCoy spokesman on behalf of the McCoy family declined the offer, saying they knew Devil Anse was never going to be returned to Kentucky or brought to justice. It wasn't about money.

Even though Devil Anse had been baptized and found the lord he never went anywhere without his rifle until the day he died. Everyone said he had gotten even more paranoid of strangers as he got older and even some of his own family. Jessie James was killed by an old friend Robert Ford in 1882, and Devil Anse was always afraid someone would try to get him the same way. He may have had quantity in years but not so much on quality.

Everyone said they never saw Devil Anse without a gun, to the contrast they said after the war they never saw Randall with a gun. Yet over the years Randall has been made out to be a Devil and Devil Anse has been made out to be a Hero. Neither could be further from the truth.

Not known if this is one of the caves Devil Anse hid in when Kentucky Law Enforcement were trying to serve the Murder Indictment Warrants on him in West Virginia. Someone should have walked by with a camera if he was in there he would have surely come out for a photo op.

Sarah McCoy

We are attempting to clarify a lot of myths and give a more in depth account of the feud. Who was one of the most influential characters of the feud other than Devil Anse and Randall McCoy? It wasn't Crazy Jim Vance or Bad Frank. It wasn't even Deadeye "Cap", Johnse or Roseanna. It was none other than Sarah McCoy, Randall's wife.

Sarah was like a silent partner in a business. She was much more than Randall McCoy's wife she was more than his best friend. She was his conscience. We will never know how many lives Sarah saved during the feud, but we're sure it was plenty. Sarah was extremely traumatized, not only from being beaten within an inch of her life but from losing seven children, her house burned to the ground, along with Roseanna getting pregnant during the feud. Her life had been difficult to say the least. It's hard to imagine the trials and tribulations she went through. She always said God can transform a tragedy into a triumph. Her attitude and love towards God never wavered. Everyone who was acquainted with Sarah had great empathy for her. Sarah always said, "When trouble overtakes you, let God take over."

Sarah was born in 1829 and married Randall Dec.9th 1849, she died in the 1890s. Sarah was a quiet woman an always tending to her own business. She was a woman who took the highroad. Everyone said she was always praying and depended on God for everything. (Sarah - Randall's wife was also my GG Grandfather Uriah McCoy's sister) Of course, Sarah was against the fighting and the hard feelings between the two families. She hated any type of friction or conflict. Sarah was the type of person who practiced what she preached, which was to honor God. Everyone said when her feet hit the floor in the morning, she would talk to God and with her last waking moment before falling off to sleep, she would talk to God. She was without a doubt a righteous woman.

Everyone who knew the McCoys always said, "had it not been for Sarah's persistence in persuading Randall not to take the law into his own hands the feud would have been much bloodier."

Randall was torn between his wife and God on one side and his sons, brothers and friends on the other. Sarah was quoted saying to Randall on more than one occasion, "vengeance is mine sayeth the Lord." On the other hand, he had Sam, Parris and Bad Frank Phillips saying an "eye for an eye, tooth for a tooth, hand for a hand and foot for a foot' also from the Bible. Bad Frank always liked adding one last remark to that, which was a life for a life and a Hatfield for each McCoy. No doubt Randall was put in a position that no one would want to be in. Should he avenge the deaths of his brother, his nephew, his four sons and daughter Alifair? Or should he continue to turn the other cheek and trust that the courts would handle Devil Anse and the other Hatfields.

Randalls initial reaction was to get his guns and head to West Virginia. Then Sarah knowing him better than Randall knew himself would comfort him. As they discussed the deaths of their children and the Godly action, they would take. More than once Randall would tell Sarah of his plans to kill Devil Anse or the others for the murders of their children. It would seem like a no-win situation. You would have thought there was no way Randall could have been talked down after Sarah would quote the scripture and explain to Randall that God must have a plan. He would then put his guns back on the rack and give in to his loving wife's request.

When Sarah was beat almost senseless by Crazy Jim Vance at the cabin massacre the doctors said, "She would never walk again or be in her right mind." Even though it was with the assistance of a cane amazingly Sarah did walk. As for her mind within a few months, she was as sharp as an arrow, which the doctors acknowledged was miraculous. Not with standing her affliction, she worked constantly dealing with the head aches from the beating she had received from the rifle butt of Crazy Jim Vance and the boot to the face from Johnse Hatfield.

Maybe Randall was a pretty good judge of character when sizing up Johnse to be his and Sarah's son n law after all. He was Devil Anses son, and the apple doesn't fall far from the tree. Naturally, after losing five children to such brutal and violent deaths she had her moments and days where she was sad. However, the other children Fanny, Adelaide and even Roseanna would gather around and listen to her tell stories of each of her children when they were babies and such. It brought joy to her to talk of them. The two of them had endured more grief than you would think is possible. Randall and Sarah never lost their faith in God and continued to read their Bible and pray daily.

As Randall and Sarah grew older, they never left each other's side. Sarah wrote a sentimental poem about each of her deceased children in her Bible and that gave her many hours of comfort. The people in Pike County were always sympatric towards the McCoys and their losses.

Randall and Sarah had talked about where "God said unto them, Be fruitful, and multiply, and replenish the earth... (Genesis 1:28)" She said it was as if Randall was questioning how they could do as God had commanded and yet Devil Anse keeps taking their children away. Once again, Sarah simply said, Ran'l, I don't have the answer to your question, but God does and that is all that matters.

After the Massacre, Sarah and Randall moved to Pikeville, where they lived out the rest of their lives. Sarah and Randall both could read and write, which was a rarity in those days. After the beating Sarah always had to wear a bonnet or hat when out in public as a chunk of her skull had been removed.

Picture above-Randall and Sarah's home in Pikeville, Kentucky.

"Preacher" Anderson Hatfield

We were always told as kids that there wasn't a more honest man than "Preacher" Anderson Hatfield that lived on the Kentucky side of the Tug River. Even though he was Devil Anse's cousin they were as different as Daylight and Dark or as opposite as their nicknames.

Preacher Anderson Hatfield was also our Great-Grandmother Nancy (Hatfield) McCoy's father. It seemed as if the Hatfield's on the West Virginia side of the Tug River were just a different breed from those on the Kentucky side. It was always said those West Virginia Hatfield's were meaner than a stripped snake. They were nothing like the Kentucky Hatfields. "Preacher" Anderson Hatfield was also the Kentucky Justice of the Peace who presided over the pig trial and also served as a prosecution witness against Devil Anse's brother Wall Hatfield at his trial.

It was always thought that "Preacher" Anse knew the pig belonged to Randall McCoy, but he wanted to please all parties involved so he chose six Hatfield's and six McCoy's to be on the jury for a reason. Everyone said Preacher Anse was playing "Solomon." His plan was to get six from each family of course each juror was going to vote for their own family. The case would be dismissed because of a hung jury. Then no one would be mad at each other or Preacher Anse because it was out of his hands. Of course, he didn't count on Drunk Bill Staton standing up and lying or Selkerk jumping ship and siding with the Hatfields.

There were actually two judges with the name of Hatfield that had connections to the feud. Wall Hatfield was the Judge in West Virginia; he presided over the Sam and Parris McCoy trail.

Randall McCoy and Preacher Anderson Hatfield just lived across Blackberry Mountain from one another. Back in those days they were practically neighbors. They never had an unkind word to say about each other. Preacher Anse was almost 80 years old when Randall McCoy died but was said to have made the journey to Pikeville to attend Randall McCoy's funeral in 1914.

Cemetery in honor of Preacher Anderson Hatfield. He was my Great Grandmothers father. Asa McCoy my Great Grandfather is buried at this cemetery located at the foot of Blackberry Mountain. Just east of where Ky 319 and Ky 1056 meet, where the pig trail was held.

Judge "Wall" Hatfield

It was Valentine "Wall" Hatfield, the brother of Devil Anse that served as a West Virginia Judge. Later, he died in a Kentucky prison for his role in the kidnapping of the three McCoys from Kentucky authorities and his role in their deaths.

On Sept. 5th 1888, Pikeville, Kentucky – the trial of Wall Hatfield was concluded, and the jury found him guilty of being an accessory to the act of murdering the three McCoys- Tolbert, Randall Jr. and Pharmer. Alexander Messer confessed to the murder of Pharmer. Both men were sentenced to the penitentiary for life.

These trials are a result of the Hatfield and McCoy Feud, which has caused so much terror on the border of Kentucky and West Virginia through the years. (It was reported in the newspapers.)

Wall Hatfield was compared to Selkerk McCoy as selling his family out. Wall, placed the blame on his brother Devil Anse. Everyone joked about how Selkerk stuck with Devil Anse and how Wall Hatfield had teamed up with Perry Cline. The two men who were once so competitive with one another were now friends.

Once Wall Hatfield had gotten away from his extremist brother Devil Anse, he saw people differently. Prior to the trial, Col. John Dil's offered to post Wall Hatfield's bond. Wall said to him, "I thought you didn't like Hatfield's" to which Col. Dils responded, "I don't like Devil Anse Hatfield but then again, tell me who does. Devil Anse has one thing on his mind, himself." Wall, did not participate in the New Year's Massacre, and the burning of the cabin, the beating of Sarah McCoy or the deaths of Randall's two other children. No doubt he regretted getting involved the last time with the three McCoy boys who were murdered.

When they were making plans for the New Year's Massacre, he advised all the men against it, and it was said he had a falling out with his brother Devil Anse over his refusal to participate. The two brothers never spoke again.

"Bad" Frank Phillips

Illustrated by Michael Hatter
Please do not copy these sketches without the written permission of Fred McCoy.

Frank Phillips, Pike County Deputy Sheriff captured at least nine Hatfield's and conspirators himself. He killed Jim Vance, Bill Dempsey and others while they were resisting arrest. Frank would often say, "seems like death is hereditary." It was like he didn't care if he took another breath or not. He was a man who had no fear of anyone or anything.

Frank was born July 27, 1861 and died July 12, 1898. He married Nancy McCoy, in Pike County, Kentucky. Nancy was the daughter of Asa Harmon McCoy and Martha Patty Cline. She was the niece of Attorney, Perry Cline. Nancy had two children with Johnse Hatfield, a boy William Anderson Hatfield name sake for his father and a girl Stella Hatfield. When she ran off with Bad Frank she took her two children with her. She married Bad Frank Phillips and had four more children. Their names were Elsie, Jesse, Flora and Golda Phillips.

Both he and Nancy had been married previously and were said to be madly in love with one another. They are buried side by side. Unlike his portrayal in the mini-series, Frank was a quiet and serious man. He was small in stature but was said to have the fortitude to tackle a grizzly bear. Bad Frank Phillips, a native of the Kentucky mountain region. In 1887 he was appointed Special Officer by the Governor of Kentucky with full arrest powers to apprehend and arrest the Hatfields on Kentucky charges and warrants. It was said he was unafraid and was a unique character. Which also earned him the nickname "Fearless Frank" as well as "Bad Frank".

Frank was an excellent shot with his cross drawn pistols. He was also good friends with Col. John Dils of Pikeville. Frank was a changed man after seeing Alifair and Calvin's bodies frozen to the ground after the massacre. Frank was quoted as saying, "God didn't mean for his children to die like that." I will seek vengeance for the way these two children were murdered. They were given no more courtesy then a man would give a coyote. Even with a name like Bad Frank he was said to have wept at the site of the Cabin Massacre.

Bad Frank started running even more raids into West Virginia, trying to arrest those he had indictment warrants on. Even though Devil Anse was hiding to far up in the mountains he did run upon Jim Vance and Cap Hatfield. Crazy Jim Vance was killed, and Cap Hatfield wounded as he turned tail and ran.

After Jim Vance was killed Devil Anse not feeling as safe from the guns of Frank Phillips moved further into the West Virginia mountains and talked about building a Fort around the family's home as he was becoming even more paranoid that Bad Frank or the McCoys were seeking their justice in the name of the children who had been murdered.

Bad Frank said I may never be able to track the Devil down, but I will show everyone what a coward he really is without his band of murderers. Devil Anse was said to have always packed his rifle around with him everywhere he went and was constantly looking over his shoulder. He may not have had to answer for the charges brought by Kentucky. He did live his life wondering if today was going to be the day that he was killed or returned to Pike County, Kentucky to stand trial for his dreadful deeds of the past. The old saying "he got away with murder" was supposed to have started, when a man was talking to a news reporter at Mate Creek. The subject had come up about Devil Anse and the many killings, he was responsible for. The man said to the reporter. "He got away with murder, pure and simple."

Frank, provided for his family after the war by becoming a bounty hunter then as a lawman. If Frank had a warrant for you, there wasn't a question of if he was coming, but when. After the 1888 Cabin Massacre and the Governor of West Virginia refuse to extradite Devil Anse and others the Governor of Kentucky appointed Frank as a Kentucky Lawman with State wide authority to capture the law breakers. It was Frank Phillips, who brought nine of those from West Virginia back to Kentucky to face trial for killing the three McCoys. It was also believed that after Frank Shot Crazy Jim Vance he tracked Cap Hatfield for several miles through the West Virginia Mountains. Several of his men in the posse had to drop out from exhaustion, but Bad Frank kept on going. He wanted revenge for the havoc "Cap" and the others had caused just a few weeks earlier at the McCoy Cabin Massacre.

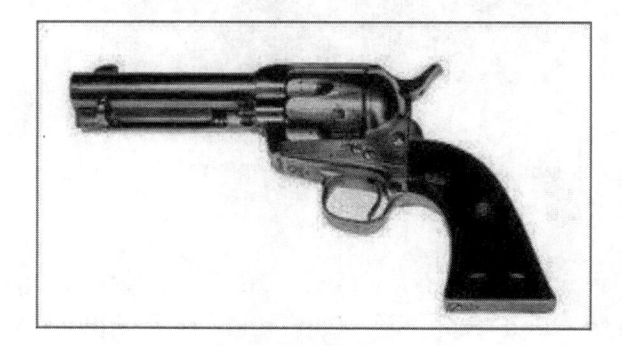

Not known if this was in fact one of Frank Phillips pistols

The Honorable
Perry Cline Esq.

Perry Cline was a prominent figure in the Hatfield McCoy Feud.

He was born on January 5, 1849 in Logan County, Virginia to Jacob "Rich Jake" Cline and Nancy Fuller. "Rich Jake" Cline was a prosperous land owner in the Tug River Valley and the second oldest son of Peter Cline. Unlike the way, he was portrayed in the most-recent movie; Perry Cline was an Honorable man to all who knew him in Pike County, Kentucky. He did, in fact, practice Law. He was a wealthy and prominent man as well.

Perry was a Lawyer, Deputy Sheriff and Deputy Jailer in Pike County, Kentucky at one time or another. He also owned thousands of acres of land. On the Kentucky side of the Tug River as well as on the West Virginia side.

Perry Cline was married in 1868 to Martha Adkins in Pike County, Kentucky. They had several children together. The most-recent movie had Perry Cline portrayed as a stalker, or pedophile with interest in Roseanna McCoy, this never happened. Anymore then the end when he was shown with the young woman and Bad Frank joked about Perry liking them young. The truth is Perry's wife was a year or two older than him. They lived a long life together, in Pike County Kentucky.

(Another Myth buster) Perry Cline was NO relation to Randall McCoy. However, he was the brother-in-law to Asa Harmon McCoy. Asa was married to Martha Patty Cline, Perry's sister. Perry was upset because Devil Anse had his brother-in-law Asa McCoy murdered, and his nephew Jeff McCoy was also murdered by a West Virginia Hatfield. There was a dispute between Perry Cline and Devil Anse over land. Perry owned land in both Kentucky and West Virginia. The land he owned in West Virginia had been given to him by his father. Perry had in inherited the land at the age of thirteen when his father had died.

Devil Anse had approximately fifty acres of land joining Perry Cline's five thousand acres. Devil Anse claimed that Perry had cut timber off his fifty acres instead of off his own five thousand acres. Perry Cine had become a lawyer after Devil Anse had swindled him out of his property. He wasn't as upset over the property that Devil Anse took as he was over his sister losing her husband Asa and his nephew being killed by Cap Hatfield. Perry Clines involvement in the perpetuation of the feud is well documented but, not always in a factual way.

Asa McCoy was friends with William H. Francis Jr. known as "Bill France." Bill was a General in the Union Army. Bill was bush wacked and shot to death by Devil Anse in 1863 in retaliation for the killing of one of his Logan Wildcats. Who at the time was stealing horses from General France. Let's not forget Devil Anse was a back woods bush whacker during the Civil War and for years after.

After watching the History Channels assessment of Perry Cline it might remind us, not to believe everything we see on TV. Giving him his due, Perry Cline, Attorney, was no different than a Police Officer; it is a job that does make enemies. As far as attorneys go he was said to be one of the most intelligent and honest around. It was only after being bamboozled at a young age by Devil Anse that he figured out he never wanted to hornswoggle anyone himself. Devil Anse had left a bad impression upon him.

Quote: *The demon of the prosecution, however, is Perry Cline, the uncle of the murdered Jeff McCoy. He is prolific of resources, patient, brave and untiring. He went into the Hatfield settlement and learned all the facts in relation to the murder of his nephew. Tall, gaunt, with long black hair and beard, with a face across which consumption's signature is written, broad and deep, he appears the very a pecure of vengeance, instead of a man trying to appease the angry demands of blood and give peace to a distracted community.*

Wheeling Intelligencer February 2, 1888
courtusyof:http://www.wvculture.org/history/hatfieldmccoyarticles.html

Randall Saves Devil Anse's Life

It was said that Devil Anse and Randall McCoy were together as they were en route to a Union Headquarters on Peter Creek. Randall knew the area better than most and was asked to lead his fellow Confederate soldiers.

It was there that Devil Anse's life was saved from an attack from two Union soldiers standing guard. After getting close to the headquarters Devil Anse went ahead to scout out the area and plan of attack. When he was bushwhacked himself, one of the union soldiers dropped out of a tree that extended over the path and knocked him off his horse and on to the ground. He was startled and couldn't move. The impact of the fall had knocked the wind clean out of him, while also either dislocating his shoulder or breaking his collar bone. Devil Anse was at their mercy. The second soldier had run up the creek bank to double team Devil Anse which was still unable to get a breath of air or defend himself. When out of nowhere Randall McCoy came riding up and hit one of the men with his horse knocking him to the ground while shooting the other killing him instantly. As Randall turned his horse around the other soldier had gotten up and raised his pistol towards Devil Anse, who was still on the ground. Randall took aim and fired striking the Union soldier in the shoulder. The Soldier then dropped his weapon, turned and ran off in the opposite direction.

The threat was over. BANG! Another shot rang out the Union Soldier is shot in the back and falls to the ground. Randall looks around confused as if what just happened. The threat was over, and the soldier was retreating. There stood Devil Anse, he had regained his composer and dropped the enemy from more than sixty yards away. By then the other Confederate soldiers arrived on the scene. Devil Anse was said to have been grateful to Randall and thanked him for saving his hide. Only a few years later Devil Anse would forget what Randall did for him and execute three of his sons. Somehow that doesn't seem to be demonstrating much gratitude.

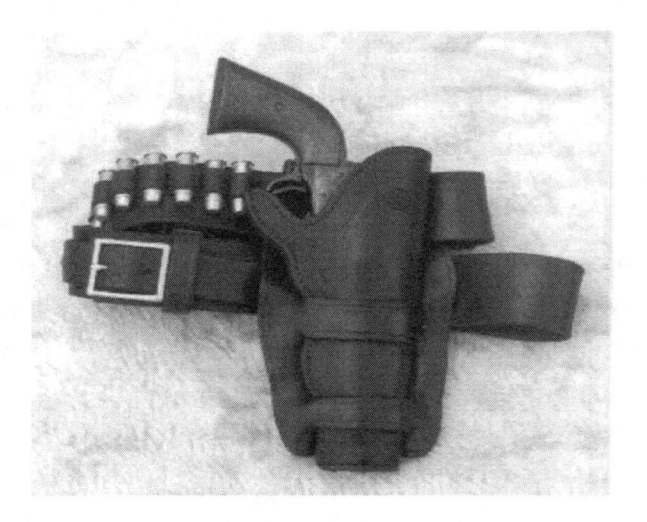

Dave Stratton

Dave Stratton was known for helping Deputies Jim McCoy and Bad Frank Phillips when they were attempting to arrest Bill Dempsey after Dempsey began shooting at the posse he was killed. Dave Stratton had been shadowing Devil Anse, waiting for the opportunity to arrest him and take him back to Kentucky to face criminal indictments there.

Dave Stratton was found unconscious near his house with massive head injuries; he died thereafter. Warrants were issued for the arrest of Devil Anse Hatfield, Cap Hatfield, Johnse Hatfield and four others. Later, it was said Mr. Stratton was struck by a train. Really? Does anyone see a pattern here? First, they say he was killed and warrants are even issued, not for one person but for seven people, and now they realize it was a train? It makes me think back to when Randall's cabin was burned with him in it, and he died a few weeks later. Sounds like the same train may have got him also.

The Real Hatfield Leader

(Crazy Jim Vance)

Some say the feud ended in 1891 after the hanging and death of Cottontop. Others say it ended with the death of Crazy Jim Vance. A lot of people thought Jim Vance was the brawn and brains behind Devil Anse. That he always told Devil Anse what to do. When the rest of the gang wasn't looking, Devil Anse and Jim Vance would have private conversations away from the others.

After Jim was killed, it all ended and Devil Anse seemed to be at a loss. He didn't know what to do next, so he ran and hid for months back and forth in the hills staying mostly in caves no doubt thinking everyday "WHY didn't I just let the law take the three McCoys on to Pikeville? Why didn't

I just let them stand trial?" He could have killed them later but because of his ego and pride, he took the law into his own hands, and it had cost him ever since.

We refer to Jim Vance many times throughout this book; the reason why is simple. He was a major player in the Hatfield and McCoy feud. Anyone who says otherwise is incorrect. Jim Vance was a mean as they come; I guess in those days it didn't hurt to be known as someone who was a little eccentric or deviated from the norm or even that he had unconventional behavior traits. In layman's terms, he was a crazy man. I have a feeling he wasn't too far from tying Cotton top for the one with the highest IQ. Even though he wasn't the brightest bulb in the room he had the nerve of a bull. Especially, when he was around the other Wildcats.

During the writing of this book, we had the privilege to talk to one of his relatives, and we shared stories we'd heard growing up in the feud country. It was amazing how similar the stories were that we had heard from our ancestors about Jim Vance. There was no one more loyal to Devil Anse then Jim Vance and with all his dirty deeds, he was also befitting of the name Devil.

Jim Vance without a doubt was mean as a snake. He died a more honorable death then Devil Anse. Shooting it out with Kentucky Law Enforcement and allowing his great nephew "Cap" to escape the long arm of the law unlike Devil Anse, he got his punishment in the end. I think he knew it was coming one day, and he embraced it for all the bad things he had done. As mean and dirty as he was he deserved more respect than that of Devil Anse Hatfield. At least he went down fighting in the end instead of hiding out in a cave.

Tolbert McCoy

In 1881, an arrest warrant was issued for Johnse Hatfield. He had been eluding arrest from Pike County Officials for months. The Pike County Sheriff had Deputized Tolbert McCoy his duties included serving warrants. Tolbert ran upon Johnse and arrested him on the warrants from Pike County, Kentucky. He was escorting Johnse to the Pike County Jail some thirty miles away. It was already late in the evening when Tolbert arrested Johnse. They had not gotten very far when who else, but Devil Anse accompanied by several members of the Logan Wildcats or Devil Anse's personal army of desperados intercepted Tolbert and Johnse. Holding Tolbert at gun point, they him relieved of his prisoner. Once again, Devil Anse had taken the law into his own hands and freed his son from the claws of justice and returned him to West Virginia. Not only were Tolbert and Jim McCoy Deputy Sheriffs for the Pike County Sheriff's Department. My brother Barry McCoy and I along with my best friend Paul Hatfield also served as Deputy Sheriffs for the Pike County Sheriff's Dept.

Jim McCoy

Two of Randall's sons were Law Enforcement officers. James "Jim" McCoy also served as a Deputy Sheriff in Pike County, Kentucky and as such arrested many murdering Hatfield's and Logan Wildcats.

Jim was born in 1850 in Logan County, West Virginia, and died 30 Aug 1929 in Pikeville, Kentucky. He married Melissa Smith February 20, 1873 in Pike Co., KY. He was in every major encounter or battle of the private war which ended when "Devil Anse" Hatfield's forces were either on the run, in hiding or dispersed by either been incarcerated, hung or killed. James (Jim) McCoy moved to Pikeville and lived quietly after the feud had ended.

The news reported in the New York Times went something like: James McCoy, 80, last of the men who actively engaged in the noted Hatfield – McCoy feud 40 years ago, died today. Jim McCoy had been converted to Christianity and had given much attention to religion in the last ten years of his life.

Devil Anse Legacy Continues

There's an old saying "If you can't get along with anybody you'd better look at yourself" this couldn't be truer when talking about some of Devil Anse or his brothers and offspring.

First, there was Devil Anse's brother big Elias he's the one who was first fighting with Tolbert McCoy at the election grounds over owing Tolbert some money. Then Devil Anse's other brother Ellison Hatfield stepped in after Tolbert had already fought with big Elias. After that fight was finished Ellison Hatfield challenged Tolbert to fight him. Ellison beat Tolbert in the head with a rock. Ellison was stabbed and shot ultimately dying.

Troy Hatfield and his younger brother also named Elias (after his uncle) have twin monuments on their graves just to the left of Devil Asne's final resting spot. It seems the "apple didn't fall too far from the tree here either. In July 1899, the 18-year-old son of Devil Anse's Hatfield Elias Hatfield named after his uncle, killed H.E. "Doc" Ellis. Evidently, Doc had filed criminal charges against Elias's brother Johnse. Being a descendant of Devil Anse it just seemed like someone had to die. Later (little) Elias and his brother Troy Hatfield another one of Devil Anse's sons seemed to carry on the Devil Anse legacy of "Bulling" but maybe this time with the wrong person.

 When dealing with the stories back then. You had three different versions of what happened. First, you had Devil Anse's version. Secondly, you had the Newspapers version. Last you "had the truth." Since I wasn't there I will just give you the basic facts as I could figure them out from reading the death reports. Basically, like their brother Johnse did most his life, Elias and Troy sold moonshine and whiskey to several of the saloons in a little town called Boomer, W.V. Just like the bloods and the Crips fighting over their turf so would Elias and Troy. Another fellow by the name of Octavio Jerome, an Italian from the same area was also dealing in the sale of alcohol to the local establishments at even lower prices than the Hatfield's. Naturally, the saloon owners wanting the better deal were buying from Jerome.

 This did not sit well with the two Hatfield brothers. They had attempted to scare him away from their area. First, they quarreled with Jerome then both of the Hatfield's beat the heck out of Jerome and left him on the side of the road. They figured if he died that would take care of their competition, and if he lived, then surely he would move to another area. Of course that didn't work. It just caused Jerome to start packing a 32 Colt Special six shot pistol. More specific a gun.

The next time the three would meet up would be their last. It seems the Hatfield's found out that Jerome had a shipment of whisky coming. Troy and (little) Elias intercepted the load of cargo. It's not sure if they kept it or just turned it away, but it did not get to its destination. After averting the delivery of Jerome's whisky the two Hatfield's went looking for Jerome to finish the job. They heard he was at a friend's house in Harewood just a short distance from Boomer.

Story goes' as they crossed the railroad track Jerome and his friend Angelo Valenzalo was setting on the porch. They saw Elias and Troy coming their way. Jerome stood up and said I won't let them two Hatfield's hurt me anymore and went inside the house. When the Hatfield's got to the porch where Jerome's friend was still sitting they ask if Jerome was there, of course the friend said he's inside. The Hatfield's took their guns out of their holsters and entered into the house. Other than those three guys inside the house there were no witnesses so it's anybody's guess as to what really happened but the result was they all three died. Each Hatfield had three gunshots to the front upper torso, and Jerome had a single gunshot to the back of his head. Elias and Troy were the first two of Devil Anse's sons to die. Devil Asne retrieved his two son's bodies and took them home to be buried. No doubt thinking all the way back to Logan County how Randall McCoy must have felt each time he had to bury one of his children.

Then, there was Montaville Hatfield, who was Devil Anse's cousin. He was sentenced to life in prison but was released some years later due to overcrowding. He was killed by his neighbor over a dispute about where the fence line should be.

Emmanuel "Willis" Wilson Hatfield, also a descendant of the famous murdering Devil Anse Hatfield and name sake of West Virginias 7th Governor E. Willis Wilson. The younger Hatfield was sentenced to the West Virginia Penitentiary in Moundsville for the murder of a Dr. Edwin O. Thornhill from Wyoming County, W.V. Reports state the physician was attending to an injured person when Hatfield asked Dr. Thornhill to issue a prescription for a pint of whiskey. The Dr. refused, and Hatfield drew his pistol and shot the Dr. twice in the chest then shot two more times into Dr. Thornhill's head as he lay on the floor dying. Hatfield then ran from the Doctors office. He was caught a few minutes later as the word spread of the good doctors death. A lynch mob was formed, and Hatfield begged the Deputies to protect him from being lynched.

Of course, we already know another one of Devil Anse's son's Deadeye William "Cap" Hatfield killed Jeff McCoy along with helping to assassinate the three McCoy Boys as well as Alifair and Cavlin McCoy. Cap like his father was an uncontrollable type fellow who always seemed to be in a battle with someone. Cap Hatfield seemed to like confrontation. Also imitating his daddy, he was outrages in his thinking. He was like the Doctor treating a person for a wart on their leg. Instead of removing the wart Cap would take the whole leg off. Actions coming from another person would have been preposterous, but coming from Cap, Devil Anse or Jim Vance it was their normal way of thinking. To them, it seemed nothing was irrational. They didn't understand the concept of "a square peg not fitting into a round hole." They had this insane way of thinking that because it was them they could do anything.

However, like Jim Vance, you would have to say that out of all the Hatfield's the one most loyal and pleasing to his father was Cap. As a son what a position to be put into when your father says to tie those boys up were going to kill them. That was his dad and he looked up to him, even if he was the Devil.

Thomas Hatfield and Ephraim Hatfield also related to the famous murderer were killed in 1902 these killings had nothing to do with the McCoy's or the feud, but it did have to do with the law. It seems Ephraim Hatfield was wanted by the Law in South Carolina. Unlike West Virginia, our Kentucky Governor honored warrants and extraditions from other states. Detective John Rutherford had gotten word that Ephraim Hatfield was hiding out at his father's house on Blackberry Creek. He got local businessman and friend Harry Watts to accompany him to Blackberry to serve the arrest warrant and send younger Ephraim back to South Carolina. Evidently, Harry Watts was a pretty well to do fellow. He owned the local Palace Hotel and several tracts of property. Det. Rutherford and Watts made their entry into the house by breaking down the door while scuffling with Ephraim, his father Thomas enters the room and begins shooting at the law. A shootout ensued when the smoke cleared all four men were dead.

Earlier in the book I mention when the West Virginia Hatfield's couldn't find anyone else to fight with they would fight with each other. Case in point is: Cap Hatfield and his brother, Elliott Hatfield were mad at each other for years. Devil Anse's only request from his death bed in 1921, was he wished that his two sons make up with each other. Cap died some years after Devil Anse of a brain tumor. It's not known if the tumors developed because of von Hippel-Lindau disease. A condition that is said to cause rage and anger in people. Cap sure seemed to have plenty of that in his life.

Troy (left) and Elias (right) Hatfield were sons of "Devil Anse." Both became involved in selling whiskey, in Boomer, W.V. they were killed on October 17, 1911 in a dispute over turf war.

Governors at Odds

Kentucky Governor S. B. Buckner

West Virginia, Governor E. **Willis Wilson**

The Hatfields and McCoys were prominent proud families who lived along the Kentucky-West Virginia borders on opposite sides of the water known as the Tug River. Both families were pioneers to the Tug Valley area. With William McCoy been the first McCoy and Ephraim Hatfield the first Hatfield.

The majority of the McCoys lived on the Kentucky side of the river while the majority of the Hatfields lived on the West Virgina side. Devil Anse the leader of the Hatfields and Randall McCoy the patriarch of the McCoy's. Both men were civil war veterans and farmers with equally large families.

The Hatfields had political clout in West Virginia with their elected officials including the Governor himself. At the height of the feud, the fighting wasn't only between the Hatfields and McCoys or their friends it was a war between the States.

Kentucky Governor S.B. Buckner (served as the 30th Governor of Kentucky) as well as E. Willis Wilson who served as West Virginas 7th Governor. The two Governors had activated troops and placed at the borders of their respective State to prepare for a "War between the States"

West Virginias Governor had accused Kentucky of kidnapping their citizens by crossing the river into West Virginia and serving arrest warrants on the Hatfields. He appealed his complaint all the way to the United States Supreme Court for a ruling. Both Kentucky and West Virginia Governors encouraged both families to move away from one another.

Randall had no choice but to move. The Hatfield's had not only burned his house down but also his brother Asa's house. The question I always ask as a child was, why was Randall encouraged to abandon his property? He wasn't the one instigating or generating any of the hostilities. It was always Devil Anse that was invading Kentucky with overwhelming numbers to intimidate and snarl at the murder charges that awaited him in Kentucky. Why, not just say let the mighty Tug River serve as the line in the sand.

In 1889, the US Supreme Court ruled against West Virginia and the Hatfield's or at least the eight that were already arrested in Kentucky. All eight stood trial and were found guilty of murder. Ellison Cottontop "Mounts" Hatfield the mentally challenged illegitimate, son of Devil Anse's Brother Ellison Hatfield, was sentenced to death and was hanged by the neck for the murder of Alifair McCoy, Randall's daughter, during the massacre in Jan. 1888, when the house was set fire. Randall's son, Calvin, was also murdered and his wife, Sarah (Sally) McCoy, was viciously and brutally beaten and left for dead.

Cottontop "Mounts" Hatfield was the only person (legally) hung during the feud and the last person to ever be hung in Pike County.

We have included a chapter on the U.S. Supreme Court's ruling for your viewing. However, some may find it boring. The bottom line is, even though they may have been brought to Kentucky against their will, now that they were here, they could be tried for their extreme and devilish crimes.

West Virginia Governor Bears Burden of Shame

Charles S. Howell, reporter wrote *five McCoys have been killed under circumstances that have few parallels in criminal history. Why then haven't these murderers been punished? Simply put it was because Governor Wilson has baffled the efforts of Kentucky Governor Buckner for their apprehension. He has had the requisition for their apprehension and extradition since September last. Repeat demands have failed to stimulate him to action in the matter. It was better in his opinion to allow the state to bear the burden of shame that she is bearing, then alienate himself from the support of one county solid Democrat.* Above is just one of the statements made by Charles S. Howell a well-spoken and stand up kind of guy. He took a lot of heat in those days for taking a stand against the Hatfield's and the Governor of West Virginia. He was the only reporter who didn't dramatize the feud. He swathe destruction first hand and wanted it to stop. He was also the only reporter whom Randall and Sarah ever had a conversation with. He was astounded that Governor Wilson of West Virginia flat out refused to honor Kentucky's extradition order and turn Devil Anse and the others over to the Kentucky Authorities to answer to the Murder charges.

Attempts to Kill Randall

The 1888 deaths of Calvin and Alifair was an irrational attempt to wipe out the McCoy's. That would have stopped Randall from striving to have the indictments served in West Virginia for the murders of his three sons in 1882 some five years previous. It would also remove the only witness (Sarah) who actually saw the three murdered boys in the custody of Devil Anse. The cabin was not the initial attempt on Randall's life; it was actually the third time his life had been in danger of ending by an assassin's bullet. The first two attempts on Randall's life were after Devil Anse, and the others had been indicted for the executions of the three McCoy boys. There was no way to get them arrested and brought back to Kentucky. As long as they stayed in West Virginia, they were safe from prosecution for the crimes they had committed in Kentucky.

Devil Anse had political power all the way up to the Governor. As long as E. Willis Wilson was Governor, no one was going to be allowed to come to his State and arrest Devil Anse. Devil Anse even named his next-to-last son after his good friend and Governor Emmanuel "Willis" Wilson. Willis Hatfield (1888-1978) was born the same year that Devil Anse ordered the McCoy's to be killed. Ironically he killed or had killed, two more of Randall's children and has a newborn of his own that he names after the Governor the very same year. Devil Anse's animosity builds towards Randall.

    Randall is on a mission he's not trying to irritate or annoy Devil Anse, he just wants to get the indictment warrants served and get justice against the men who had executed his three sons. The Hatfield's heard that Randall and Calvin going to make a trip to Pike County the next day to inquire as to why Devil Anse, and his band of murderers had not been arrested.

    When Devil Anse got word of this, he planned to bushwhack Randall and his son. It just so happened that Randall and Calvin got a late start and was running behind. Luck is not something Randall had a lot of, but on this day, God was watching over him. His two neighbors (Scott's) were also going to Pikeville that same day and had gotten an earlier start, traveling in the same direction as Randall and his boy. The story goes that they were fired upon from several snipers within the woods. Both their horses were killed, and one of the Scott's was injured. Lo and behold the assassins shot at the wrong people. Had Randall been on time and not running late it could have been him and Calvin, and they may not have missed.

    The second assassination attempt was when Randall was at his cabin standing in the doorway early one morning and looking towards his boys grave on the opposite side of the hill. The three boys were buried in the same grave, side by side but in three separate coffins. He was pondering on how he missed his boys when a single gunshot rang out from high upon the hill. The bullet hit the door facing and lodged in the wood. It would remain there as a reminder of the hatred the Hatfield's had for him until the "New Year's Eve Massacre," and the cabin was burned to the ground. That's why there have always been questions as to how Randall McCoy actually died in 1914. Everyone knew there was a fire but there were other fires over the course of the fighting. The Hatfield's had burned down Asa Harmon's cabin where Jim McCoy was holding Johnse after arresting him for selling moonshine, on the night Roseanna rescued him. They burned Randall's cabin down on the "New Year's Eve Massacre" and now he dies from a fire as well. Really? To bad we didn't have CSI back then because the ending may have been different.

There were those who had made vows and promises that one day they would kill Randall McCoy to avenge the death of Crazy Jim Vance, Ellison Hatfield, and Wall Hatfield; Devil Anse's other brother who died in prison. Was it in fact, a freak accident or did Devil Anse or "Cap" actually keep their promise that they would one day kill Randall McCoy. Of course, we know that Devil didn't do it himself; surely he was home sick in bed as always, with someone else doing his dirty work.

Just like back in 1886 when Cap Hatfield and Jim Vance had Jeff McCoy tied up on the West Virginia side of the Tug River. Crazy Jim untied Jeff McCoy's hands and told him if he could swim to the Kentucky side, they would let him go.

Jeff McCoy was Asa McCoy's son and also Perry Cline and Randall McCoy's nephew. They took him to the deepest part of the Tug and let him go. He did swim to the other side of the river where his mother Martha McCoy, and his sister Nancy were waiting. As he was climbing up the river bank thinking, he was safe from the clinches of the Hatfield's a shot ring out, Cap using a Rifle shot him dead right there on the Kentucky River bank in front of his mother and sister. Jeff and his uncle Perry Cline was extremely close after Asa was killed Perry Cline had assumed the job of caring for his sister and her children. Jim and Cap laughed and carried on about what a good shot it was. This was the reason Perry Cline disliked the West Virginia Hatfield's so much. Not over land but for the murder of his brother n law and his nephew. Notice, how all the murdering took place on the Kentucky side, they knew that West Virginia's Governor Wilson would not sign extradition papers for any of them to be turned over to Kentucky. They knew they were safe. Devil Anse had one of the largest voting families in West Virginia. He practically ruled Logan County, and Devil Anse's family had always supported Gov. Wilson.

Myths

Myth #1 –

- When the Hatfields surrounded Randall McCoys House on New Year's Eve 1887, Randall ran and hid in the pig pin while his family was been slaughtered.

TRUTH-

Randall McCoy was a seasoned war veteran. This is not the deserter we're talking about here. This is a man who stayed the course and fought when he could have deserted with Devil Anse Hatfield, Ellison Hatfield, Elias and even Anse's cousin young Ephraim Hatfield.

This myth couldn't be further from the truth. Randall wasn't afraid of Jim Vance or the West Virginia Hatfield's. It was they who were afraid of Randall. Why else would a band of at least nine (started out with thirteen) outlaws attack a man's home in the middle of the night and set fire burning his home to the ground with his wife and children inside. With at least two of them having special needs or physically handicapped.

That's where Devil Anse's lies to the media were so misleading. Devil Anse himself knew what type man Randall was, that's why he was always sending others to do his dirty work. He had seen first-hand in combat what Randall was capable of.

That's the very reason everyone said the feud could have been so much worse, but Sarah and God kept Randall in check. The ole saying "walk softly and carry a big stick" couldn't have been truer than with Randall. He wasn't a bragging man. He knew what he was capable of and evidently so did Devil Anse and his army of outlaws.

Who could have predicted what a coward like Devil Anse and an idiot like Jim Vance would do.

Jim Vance was the man that had been accused of things so bad and immoral we won't even print them in our books. Who would have thought they would stoop so low as to set the cabin on fire and start executing the children as they came out or beat a 62 year old woman with a gun and leave her for dead.

They were afraid with Randall's background; he may have had a trap set for just the occasion of uninvited guests. They saw Randall wasn't giving up and knew that by killing and beating three more members of his family they had done nothing more than make him even more angry. When Randall came out of the house with his shotgun and both barrels blazing they knew it was time to leave. Nine men against one and they are the ones running, with at least three of them shot and wounded. Then Devil Anse starts the rumor that Randall ran. That sounds different from the stories that have been told for years. Don't take our word "do the research**.**" Read the statements of those that were captured. They were the cowards -- not Randall McCoy.

Myth #2-

Ref. Bill Staton:

- Bill Staton –was murdered two months after Pig Trial by both Sam **and** Paris McCoy

TRUTH-

*Staton was killed over two and a half years **after** the pig trial.

*He was killed **(**not murdered**)**

*He was killed in self-defense not revenge.

*Sam McCoy shot Bill Staton.

*Paris was unable to shoot; Bill had just shot him in the **back.**

*Then Sam killed Bill Staton.

*His death was ruled **self-defense** by a Hatfield judge in West Virginia.

Myth #3-

Why would a grown man want to make such a fuss over a pig? He (Randall) just wanted to cause trouble.

TRUTH-

Principle, Honesty, Integrity, and **Accountability**. The list goes.

Let's review, this is a man who watched Devil Anse, and two of Anse's brothers desert the army even-though he chose to stay and fight. He's taken prisoner and no doubt thought about Devil Anse being home with his family while he is being held captive.

Then he's released, comes home and finds out his brother has been murdered by the Hatfield's or the Hatfield's gang. Now another Hatfield has a pig that belongs to him. You may have heard the old expression "the straw that broke the camel's back", well the pig just happened to be the straw. It was just more than Ole Ran'l could bear.

First of all, we're talking about a huge family here with a lot of mouths to feed and that was food taken from his children, but that wasn't the real issue here. Randall just wanted the Hatfield's to be held accountable.

The pig itself wasn't the problem at all; it was that he was tired of being pushed around. Randall just wanted to be left alone but every time he turned around something was happening and it usually involved Devil Anse or his family.

Myth #4-

- Ellison Hatfield was stabbed <u>26-32</u> times. And shot 1-6 times
- (GET REAL!)

TRUTH-

Tolbert McCoy had nothing more than a small bladed knife (what we call a pocket knife today) he used around the farm. The blade was said to be no longer then a man's finger. Devil Anse Hatfield's family was the only ones to see the wounds because they loaded Ellison up and headed back to West Virginia.

According to the stories that were told during that time, he may have had <u>6 – 7 stab</u> wounds at the most. (Of course either Devil Anse Hatfield or the newspaper figured it sounded better with the 26-32 stab wounds but that was <u>NOT</u> the truth.) (How hard is it to take a knife and make tears in a shirt after the fact?) Now days it's called tampering with evidence.

"Do the math" if he had actually had 26 -32 knife wounds there would have been no reason for a gun shot.

Maybe after Devil Anse killed the three McCoy's (one of which was totally innocent) and realizing what he had done, he figured they had best make it look as bad as they could. We don't know. We weren't there. In all reality, would any of us stand around while three men jumped onto one person, especially while they are stabbing him? Doesn't matter what his last name is. As high strung as the West Virginia Hatfield's were, there would have been twenty Hatfields on top of the McCoys.

There was no CSI back then but let's use some common sense here. First, if someone had been stabbed 26-32 times, even with a pocket knife, would he still be fighting like everyone had confirmed Ellison was? 26-32 times and still had to shoot him! I have seen some tough men in my life time but that's a little hard to buy. As an investigator I just don't see it. Have nothing to go on except experience, logic, and research on stab wounds over the years.

- It's like the Loch Ness Monster or Bigfoot, the stories continued to grow from person to person.
- **Two reasons for this rumor:**
- **Number 1** - Devil Anse executed three boys tied to trees and one of them was without a doubt totally innocent.

- **Number 2** - In my professional opinion the outrageous amount of stab wounds that were reported were a smoke screen for the execution of the McCoy's. Or the news media created the idea in order draw more attention to the story.

Myth #5-

- In an era when Asa Harmon McCoy's military service was an act of disloyalty, even his family believed the man had brought his murder on himself.

TRUTH-

We all know Randall was not pleased with Asa Harmon joining the Union but this was his younger brother. Randall loved his brother and family. No way did he want him harmed, Union or Confederate.

Myth #6-

- Randall McCoy was mad because Devil Anse Hatfield had cut timber off Randall's property.
- McCoy's were trying to steal timber rights from Devil Anse

TRUTH-

Randall McCoy never owned any property in West Virginia. Why would Randall be mad at Devil Anse over timber?

The feud had to do with a lot of things but timber on Randall's part, was not one of them. (Randall was a farmer he didn't cut timber) There was absolutely no dispute between Randall and Devil Anse over property or timber.

No one ever heard about timber until years after the feud. Devil Anse used the myth of a land dispute as nothing more than a red herring.

Truth is Devil Anse Hatfield's property was located in West Virginia. Randall McCoy's property was located in Kentucky. This is just another myth that over the years took a life of its own. It's not true.

Myth #7-

- Three of Randall's sons killed Devil Anse's brother Ellison.

TRUTH-

Only Ellison and Tolbert were fighting at first, from the stories I always heard growing up, Ellison was really hurting or going to hurt Tolbert with a large rock. At that point Pharmer jumped in, not really trying to fight but to separate the two. As Pharmer was attempting to separate them, other's also joined in, attempting to stop the fight that had now turned into a brawl.

The story goes' in different directions here as to how bad Ellision was hurting or going to hurt Tolbert. What is undisputed is Pharmer shot Ellison. The third brother, Randall McCoy Jr. was totally innocent. He was only trying to help separate the two who were fighting. In fact some said it wasn't even Randall Jr. that it was William McCoy his brother trying to pull the two apart. When the gun went off they just happen to grab Randall Jr. instead of William.

Myth #8-

- Randall McCoy was always being interviewed by the media, and promoting the feud.

Truth-

This couldn't be further from the truth. Randall McCoy never gave interviews or talked to the media. He didn't want to promote the feud. However, by not talking to the media the stories became one sided and left the McCoy's open to bad stories or print. By Randall not responding to the press, everyone had to accept the stories that Devil Anse told as the truth.

One news reporter who Randall had asked to leave his property wrote, "He's a sad man and never smiles". Randall's home had been burnt and his wife had been beaten, he had five children murdered, a brother murdered, a nephew murdered, a grandbaby to die, Rosanna (his daughter) and son William had passed away. Maybe at that time in his life there wasn't a lot to smile about.

The most recent movie showed Randall on a front porch posing with a rifle for a newspaper picture. **It Never Happened!** Devil Anse is the one who welcomed the media and the attention it brought. He was always posing for pictures, even handing out guns to his small children to be photograph in order to enhance the photo. Don't take my word for it Google Hatfield and McCoy pictures and see how many pictures of Devil Anse and his clan show up. It was Devil Anse who welcomed the attention "Not Randall".

Why do you think there are only a couple of pictures of Randall out there? He never took a picture or allowed anyone else to.

Imagine you're a news reporter from New York and your editor says to you, "Go to Kentucky and get a story on those crazy feuding Hillbilly's, the Hatfields and McCoys." Then you make the trip to Kentucky upon arriving you ask Randall McCoy for pictures and a story and he has nothing to say, except asking you to leave his property.

After leaving Randall you go to Devil Anse who was no doubt a business man and the reporter tells Anse, "I have got to get pictures and a story for my editor." Devil Anse agrees for pay or not but he agrees to do a story. In your opinion who do you think the story is going to favor. The one who told you to get off his property or the one who gave you a story and saved your job. It may have been all lies that Devil Anse told him but to the reporter it was an assignment completed.

I agree its Randall's own fault for not talking, but the point is everyone was only getting one side of the story and it was coming from a man who was as sly as a fox. They said Devil Anse knew more ways to take your money than a room full of lawyers.

Myth #9-

- Randall fought for the Union. Devil Anse fought for Confederacy

TRUTH-

Both clan leaders along with my Great Grandfather, Uriah McCoy fought for the Confederacy. There was even a time when they all fought together. Randall did in fact save Devil Anse's life in one battle. Devil Anse was said to have been grateful to Randall. Family members from the Hatfields and McCoys fought on both sides during the Civil War.

Myth #10-

- Devil Anse was said to have been ordered to execute his uncle and one of his uncle's friends who had taken leave without permission in order to visit the friends dying wife. It was because of this order that Devil Anse decided to desert the war rather than to carry out this order.

TRUTH-

WOW! I expect to hear anytime that a reporter wrote a story on how Devil Anse could walk on water! There is absolutely **NO** proof to back this outrageous statement up. Again all the deserters were trying to save face when returning home after deserting from their obligation. This was just another tall tale.

Myth #11-

- Cottontop shot Alifair at the New Year's Eve Massacre.

TRUTH-

According to Fanny McCoy and her mother Sarah McCoy in their court testimony, Cap Hatfield is the one who shot Alifair as she left the cabin to fetch some water to put out the fire. Cottontop, after seeing that he may have got the "short end of the stick", (or should I say rope) in his own testimony said, "The Hatfield's made me do it".

Myth #12-

- Crazy Jim Vance was murdered.

TRUTH-

Crazy Jim Vance wasn't murdered—He was killed. Frank Phillips had Kentucky Arrest Warrants for Jim Vance, Cap Hatfield, Devil Anse Hatfield, and others. When he happened upon Crazy Jim and Cap, they opened fire on Frank and his posse. Frank and the posse returned fire and Cap Hatfield ran. It was easy to set fire to a cabin and kill a disabled girl but get in a gun fight with real men and he ran. Crazy Jim Vance was killed.

Note: No one shined their shoes with his brains and no one stuck their finger inside his head and then into their mouth. These are all myths maybe even created by the Devil himself. You have to give Devil Anse his due. He ran an effective public relations campaign against the McCoy's and in favor of the Hatfield's. Then again, how hard could that have been when he was the only one talking to the press? Especially, when Devil Anse was known for being so windy he could "blow up an onion stack". When a person can kill another man's children and get the focus turned so the victim in fact looks like the perpetrator that's an effective publicity campaign.

Myth #13-

Devil Anse did not want to be notorious and famous when taking all the pictures with his family holding guns. He just got played by the reporters.

TRUTH-

Devil Anse was a legend in his own mind. He seemed to love the attention and posing for reporters. If he didn't like all the reporters, all he had to have done was the same as Randall McCoy did every time a reporter came to his door. Randall always ask them to leave and said he had nothing to say. Other than the one time he told a reporter, "The more you stir it, the more it's going to stink."

Myth #14-

- After the cabin massacre and two more of Randall and Sarah's children were murdered, Sarah told Randall to "go do what he had to do."

TRUTH-

Not true at all. At no time was it ever said that Sarah wanted to seek revenge for the death of her children. Of course her heart was broken but she only prayed more and kept assuring Randall that God would see them through the hard times.

Myth or Not- don't really know on this question?

Was Randall McCoy Jr. aka (Bud) taken by mistake by the Hatfield's in place of his brother

William "Bill" McCoy who was really the third McCoy attempting to get Ellison off Tolbert when they were fighting?

My Thoughts-Don't know the answer to this, in the end it really wouldn't have mattered Devil Anse would still have murdered an innocent person. From all witness accounts all the third McCoy had done was attempt to separate the two men who were fighting.

Myth #15-

- Randall McCoy said Devil Anse was six foot and one hundred eight pounds of pure hell.

Truth-

Why would Randall say that? Randall thought Devil Anse was a coward. He thought that about him when he witnessed him deserting the army. He thought he was a coward for the way he tied his three boys to trees and shot them. He thought he was a coward when he sent the Logan Wildcats to kill Asa Harmon. He thought he was a coward when he sent the Logan Wildcats to burn his house down and kill him and his family. No we were never told Randall thought Devil Anse was anything other than a coward, so this too would be a myth. Besides as far as the size of the two men Randall was a much larger man then Devil Anse was. Saw in a book a few years back where this same saying was attributed to Cap Hatfield instead of Devil Anse.

Myth#16- Randall McCoy was jealous of Devil Anse.

Truth-

Lets use some common since here. When Randall married Sarah they had a 300 plus acre farm on Blackberry Fork now known as Hardy. At this time Devil Anse owned 50 acres in West Virginia. Then they both went off to war. When they return Randall continues farming and by the time the feud begins has over a hundred head of cattle, several sheep, chickens and of course many pigs. He raises corn for his cattle; remember that is where Calvin was attempting to run to the night of the cabin massacre, (corn crib). For a farmer, Randall and his family done ok.

If you recall the first fight at the election grounds was with Elias and Tolbert and what was it over? Money! Who owed who, money? Elias Hatfield owed Tolbert McCoy money for a fiddle. Now as an investigator why would the McCoys be jealous of the Hatfields at this point in life? The Hatfields owed the McCoys money. Truth is during the feuding years neither family had a lot. The feud wasn't over jealousy as Devil Anse wanted everyone to believe years later. Of course twenty years after the feud Devil Anse became a wealthy man from his timbering business. This was many years after the feud had ended. After Randall had lost half his family his goal in life was just to survive without losing any more children. He never had a goal of fame or fortune unlike his counter.

    During the feud no one ever reported on the hundred or so cows that were shot or stolen from the McCoy's not to mention pigs that were mutilated and left to rot in the fields. Of course when you have children being executed it's not very important to complain about your livestock it's just not that important in comparison to your family being slaughtered. I think jealousy was the last thing on Randall McCoy's mind.

U.S. Supreme Court

MAHON v. JUSTICE, 127 U.S. 700 (1888)

127 U.S. 700

MAHON
v.
JUSTICE, Jailer, etc.

May 14, 1888

127 U.S. 700 (1888)

MAHON
v.
JUSTICE.

No. 1411.

Supreme Court of United States.

Argued April 23, 24, 1888.
Decided May 14, 1888.
APPEAL FROM THE CIRCUIT COURT OF THE UNITED STATES FOR THE DISTRICT OF KENTUCKY.

Mr. *J. Proctor Knott* for appellee.

MR. JUSTICE FIELD, after stating the case as above reported, delivered the opinion of the court.

The governor of West Virginia, in his application on behalf of the State for the writ of *habeas corpus* to obtain the discharge of Mahon and his return to that State, proceeded upon the theory that it was the duty of the United States to secure the inviolability of the territory of the State from the lawless invasion of persons from other States, and when parties had been forcibly taken from his territory and jurisdiction to afford the means of compelling their return; and that this obligation could be enforced by means of the writ of *habeas corpus,* as the court in discharging the party abducted could also direct his return to the State from which he was taken, or his delivery to persons who would see that its order in that respect was carried out.

If the States of the Union were possessed of an absolute sovereignty, instead of a limited one, they could demand of each other reparation for an unlawful invasion of their territory and the surrender of parties abducted, and of parties committing the offence, and in case of refusal to comply with the demand, could resort to reprisals, or take any other measures they might deem necessary as redress for the past and security for the future. **But the States of the Union are not absolutely sovereign. Their sovereignty is qualified and limited by the conditions of the Federal Constitution. They cannot declare war or authorize reprisals on other States. Their ability to prevent the forcible abduction of persons from their territory consists solely in their power to punish all violations of their criminal laws committed within it, whether by their own citizens or by citizens of other States.**

Basically, what I gathered from the U.S. Supreme Court's ruling is:

First, one state cannot declare war on another State. Of course this had almost happened between Kentucky and West Virginia by the two Governors.

Secondly, even if the person in question was brought back to Kentucky on a legal Kentucky Arrest Warrant, if he refused to consent to being returned back to the state in which the warrant was issued and went against his will it would be considered kidnapping.

The recourse would be to charge the person who brought him back across state lines criminally in the state he was abducted from.

Since Devil Anse was friends with the Governor of West Virginia there was no other way to get those indicted back to Kentucky to answer the murder charges.

Being that Governor E. Willis Wilson refused allow the extradition of those charged to Kentucky. The way I also understand it is that even though you could charge (Frank Phillips) with the kidnapping of those he had brought back to Kentucky on Criminal Indictment Warrants. They were now on Kentucky soil and could be arrested and charged legally on those same Warrants, and <u>they were.</u>

The whole thing between the two states was pretty simple, had not the Governor of West Virginia let his friendship with the Devil get in the way of him doing his job and duty as Governor, and at the request of the Kentucky Governor simply turn over (All) (Devil Anse Included) **those named in the Murder Indictments to Kentucky to answer to the murder charges.**

 Seems the whole reason for the Appeal to the U.S. Supreme court by Governor Willis Wilson was to protect Devil Anse, it wasn't about Mahorn but he knew if Frank Phillips or others were allowed to come into West Virginia and take Mahorn then they could just as easily come and Arrest Devil Anse on the same warrants.

Now that Frank Phillips knew it was illegal to enter West Virginia and Arrest on Kentucky warrants even for murder charges it gave Devil Anse piece of mind knowing as long as he stayed out of Kentucky he couldn't be touched.

"Monument for a Murderer"

The Devil Exposed

"Devil Anse" Hatfield ordered this marble statue of himself before his death, it was carved in Italy, he had it hauled up the mountainside by mules.
(According to Life Magazine May 22nd 1944)

Devil Anse walked away from the war and left his men behind not giving a second thought to their survival. Devil Anse returned home and he collected deserters, thieves, renegades and desperados together to form "The Logan Wildcats". These were men who couldn't or didn't want to make it in the military.

A lot of people didn't even know these men had deserted. Family and friends assumed and the deserters told them they had returned to the area for home front security. We could find no official documentation stating that William Anderson Hatfield was ever commission as a Captain in the Confederate Army.

On his monument, it says Captain, but we know he was not a Captain in the Confederate Army. Our guess is his uncle Jim Vance gave him this title. Maybe it's related to his gang of outlaws the Logan Wildcats with no connection to the military (Jim Vance already gave himself the title of Capt.). If Devil Anse was commissioned a Captain in the Confederate Army and then deserted, he would have lost that title and commission? Our thoughts on this subject are that after a couple of shots of Johnse's moonshine, "Captain" Jim Vance says, "Hey Anse you're a Captain too!"

Randall knew Devil Anse's band of deserters had murdered his brother. It was said the Logan Wildcats were like a bunch of dogs or wolves running in a pack. They felt protected in numbers. Several Wildcats to one man and that's how they liked it. That's what they would call an "even fight." Assassinating or shooting someone in the back, it didn't matter to the Wildcats, as long as they came out on top.

In West Virginia and Kentucky the name Hatfield meant terror. Devil Anse ravaged the state of West Virginia and Kentucky. There was a saying from those who knew or lived near the Hatfields "to offend a Hatfield is the surest form of suicide." If the Hatfields had a grudge against a man, they would hunt him until his death. If someone had done to another family what Devil Anse did to Randall McCoy's family in modern times, people would be totally outraged. Nevertheless, Devil Anse has always been portrayed as some kind of hero when in reality he was nothing more than a murderer. He was not only a murderer but a murderer who went unpunished for his crimes.

Let's put the war, the pig, the love affair to the side and let's just talk about the killings and the lives that were lost during the feud. Devil Anse or the men under his control murdered: Asa Harman McCoy, Tolbert and Pharmer McCoy killed Ellison Hatfield; Devil Anse kidnapped and executed three McCoy boys. Cap Hatfield murdered Jefferson McCoy. Sam McCoy killed Bill Staton, Devil Anse then says, "Let's kill them all" and has murdered Calvin McCoy and Alifair McCoy (two more of Randall's children as they run out of the burning cabin), and savagely and brutally beat Randall's wife Sarah and leaves her for dead on the ground. Bad Frank Phillips kills Jim Vance. The Justice System kills Cottontop. Where was Devil Anse Hatfield's Punishment?
He runs up into the mountains and hides. It seems Devil Anse wanted punishment for everyone except himself.

Then there's a monument to honor him. Would "deserter" on his monument have received as much admiration and attention as Captain has?

When I was a kid around (12 years old) I remember my dad and mom owning Blackberry Super Market, a little country store on Blackberry Creek, just a little ways up the road from the election ground. There was an article in the local newspaper that was talking about the statue of Devil Anse. Just like any country store, you always had those loafers that would come in sit around the stove and trade coon hunting stories or maybe even an occasional knife. On this particular day, there was an article in the newspaper about Devil Anse's monument, and it showed a picture of it. One of the loafers made a comment about what a big monument it was. I remember one of the other guys saying a, "Monument for a Murderer." That comment has stuck with me all my life.

As I got older and heard more stories and researched the feud, I started thinking Devil Anse was a murderer. He killed or had people killed. Devil Anse was never brought to justice. He either hid or traveled in large groups for protection. I want the record straight, and the truth told on both sides. I'm as much Hatfield as I am McCoy. I was recently reading a clip from a newly released book, and that's what made me decide that someone in the McCoy family had to correct some of the myths. The author wrote, "Devil Anse is said to have single handily fended off a company of Union solders." Wow! I guess Devil Anse was a one-man army. (Note: Army Company consisted of 100 soldiers.) I wish book authors, and movie producers would research some of their stories and use some common sense. Devil Anse was not a hero during the war or the feud; in fact, his nickname speaks volumes. Drop the (D) and it will tell you more about his character, "EVIL". Just telling it like it is, without the Hollywood touch.

As I have said many times our great-grandmother was "Preacher" Anderson Hatfield's Daughter, two of my dad's sister's married two Hatfield brothers. They were two of the finest men I have ever known. My best friend and partner Detective, as well as a fellow Police Chief for many years is a Hatfield. I am only referring to Devil Anse and the men who set fire to cabins and killed and beat women and children.

There were no hero's during this feud, and if there was it definitely wasn't Devil Anse Hatfield. For years, the monument has been revered as that of a war hero or an acclaimed individual who had excelled in life as a humanitarian, or excelled during a war befitting such a display for recognition of their good deeds or service. Devil Anse deserted the war and in no way was he a humanitarian.

The monument would be fitting for a President or dignitary, but not that of a Murderer.

Pattern of Behavior

It seems like all through Devil Anse's life he was in a conflict with someone, and it usually involved timber, livestock or some other form of property. He seemed to be a very possessive kind of man. If you do the research and look at any lawsuits filed over timber and property you will see the pattern. Furthermore, I have watched documentaries over the years about the Hatfields and McCoys feud. I often hear the narrator say Devil Anse, and Randall fought over timber and property.

That's just not so they never had any disputes over property or timber. Devil Anse had disputes and court cases with many people over the years. Not one time was he or Randall in court over property or timber rights. Randall always got along well with his Kentucky neighbors, Hatfields and otherwise. There is absolutely no evidence, documentation or proof that supports the rumors they had any conflicts or issues over property. It was as if Devil Anse was paranoid that someone was always trying to steal his property and constantly in court against someone.

Even today people don't like appearing in court. They may have just said you can have it. It's just not worth fighting over. Back in those days property was plentiful with small populated areas. Devil Anse didn't really want the land, just the timber off of it, he may have struck a deal and settled for the timber, the property owner got to keep his land. Who knows why Devil Anse did the things he done? How all the rumors, started on Randall makes you think maybe the jealousy everyone has talked about over the years was on the part of Devil Anse and not Randall.

    People are not always envious of others because of belongings. Devil Anse may have been jealous of Randall because of his Military service, his morals, or his family. There could have been so many reasons he resented Randall. The bottom line is, there is not one shred of evidence that Randall McCoy ever did anything wrong or dishonest to Devil Anse, before, during or after the feud. Of course, the boys killing Ellison was wrong. However, that was not Randall's fault. Anyone who has children knows that they don't always listen to their parents. Nor do they always make the right decision and choices in life. In this case, the bad judgment they showed cost them their lives. Devil Anse never did pay.

Brother against Brother

Over the years, the Hatfield's always wanted it to appear that Asa Harmon McCoy fought for the Union, and the McCoy family as a result disowned him. However, what was never reported is that there were four Hatfield's that fought for the Confederacy who also fought in the feud but there were many more of Devil Anse's kin folk who just like Asa McCoy fought for the Union.

Remember the Civil War wasn't just a "War Between the States" but sometimes a war that pitted brother against brother.

Job

The Faith of Job

The first time I ever heard of Job in the Bible was when my grandmother was talking about Randall McCoy losing most of his family, in one way or another. During the feud, she said Randall had the faith of Job and that no matter how bad things got for Randall, he never lost his faith. She also attributed this to his wife Sarah "Keeping him in line" as she put it.

Why would a producer of a movie degrade a person the way the History Channel did to Randall McCoy in the last hour of the movie? He suffered enough while he was alive, and now they have to slander his name and faith. We were born and raised on Blackberry Creek and have heard many stories all our lives about the feud and in all those years we never at any time, not even once, heard anyone say Randall cursed God. He never lost his faith. All the man had left was his faith.

We have wanted to tell the truth about some things for years but held back. Since a movie about the feud showed such disregard for the truth we felt we had to tell it now. The sad thing is, if people liked the movie so much the way it was, imagine if the movie producers did a little research and filmed the feud the way it really happened.

The Hatfield-McCoy feud is a legend; few true and authentic facts have been printed about it up until now. The surviving McCoys of the day were close-mouthed, but no more.

Book Recommendations

Maybe it's where I have the same last name of Randall but two of the best books I have read dealing with the feud are: Truda McCoy's –The McCoy's Their Story and my brother Barry McCoy's book, The Story of the McCoy's you can go to www.barrymccoy.com to order yours. We both took different approaches when writing our books.

Some of the stories Devil Anse told throughout the years to reporters and such was nothing more than lies. The reporter's stories had been fabricated, stretched, or were totally false, but it didn't matter to them because they only needed a story.

Hatfield & McCoy Feud
"The Story of the McCoy's"
By Barry McCoy

www.barrymccoy.com

Nicknames

The Hatfield's and McCoy's had nicknames as did a lot of mountain people.

Ole Ran'l —Randall McCoy was called Ole Ran'l" because he was the oldest man in his Company when serving with the Confederate Army. A lot of the men looked up to him as a father figure. They started out calling him Old Man. Then one day when one of the officers needed someone local who knew the area for advice on an upcoming battle they were preparing for, one of the men said to ask Ole Ran'l and the name stuck with him.

Devil Anse- Anderson Hatfield's mother tagged him with that name as a child when he was growing up for being so mean.

"**Cottontop**" – Ellison (Mounts) Hatfield received this name for his white hair. They also called him Half Wit: because he was mentally retarded.

Cap Hatfield or Deadeye - William Hatfield was named "Cap" for the white cap that covered his eyeball from an injury as a child. He also had a second nickname given to him by the Logan Wildcats. They called him dead eye as a joke referring to his shooting ability. They said the gang always wanted Cap or dead eye out in front of everyone that he had once shot another member of their gang in the back of the neck during a raid. The joke was Cap was blind in one eye and couldn't see out of the other.

"Bad" Frank Phillips - because he was "badder" then a junk yard dog, or as most called him back in those days. He was "Bad to the Bone" and it was a known fact that Devil Anse feared him.

"Big Sam" or Squirrel Huntin' Sam McCoy – His nickname is pretty much self-explanatory. He was big and the best around at hunting squirrels.

Crazy Jim Vance- No one's name was more fitting than that of Crazy Jim Vance's. He was as crazy and ruthless as they come.

Making a Mountain out of a Mole Hill

Contrary to what Devil Anse and the History Channel would have you believe Randall and Sarah lived as happy a life as two people could, considering the tragedies and the devastation they had endured.

If anyone who has an interest in the feud would just play detective and look at the facts you can uncover a lot of the lies that have been told over the years. Going back to where a reporter once said, "Randall was jealous of Devil Anse." Let's consider the evidence. If you have ever seen pictures of Randall McCoy's cabin before it was burnt to the ground you would have seen that there were two adjoining cabins. It was a beautiful home.

Even when Randall moved he had bought one of the largest houses in Pikeville. (See picture) Remember he had a huge family even though he had lost seven children. Look at Uriah McCoy's house (see picture) in Burnwell, Kentucky where Roseanna lived for a while. These are not shabby houses, especially back in the 1800s. Nothing personal (investigating objectively) look at these homes.

Then look at devil Anses and decide for yourself who had more reasons to be jealous. Maybe that's why they always burnt the McCoy homes down. Bottom line is, we hope all parties involved are at peace in heaven together. It was a shame that any of it happened, however, let's not forget the facts; Randall McCoy never went to West Virginia after the Hatfield's. It was always them who came to Kentucky.

Randall McCoy never did one thing in retaliation against Devil Anse or his family. Randall didn't want his daughter to marry Johnse. The truth is what father is ever happy with the guy, who's going to take his daughter away. I don't think the last name of Hatfield had as much to do with it as everyone wants to believe. People love a good Romeo and Juliet story, that's what the media made Roseanna and Johnse out to be.

Bottom line is, Johnse had a reputation as being a ladies man. Roseanna's dad knew that and he was just trying to save her from some heart ache. As any father knows sometimes what we think is best for our child isn't. Randall loved his daughter as much as any of the children. Any parent knows we don't just quit loving our children when they disobey.

Painful Memories

Over the years, I've read stories where someone said they were on the ferry boat in Pikeville and that Randall was talking about the Hatfields to anyone who would listen. That couldn't be farther from the truth. It just didn't happen. Everyone in the McCoy family always said Randall didn't talk during or after the feud and the McCoys in general didn't either. (I guess my brother, and I are making up for everyone else for years past).

In the front of this book, we wrote about Randall and the McCoys being stubborn that never changed. Randall never discussed the feud with anyone other than the McCoy Family. Why would he want to talk about it very much to anyone? It was bad enough he, and his family had to live the nightmare. Why would he talk about it?

Practice What You Preach

A preacher was talking with Randall and Sarah while sitting on their front porch of their new home in Pikeville about how rough things must have been with them losing seven of their children.

Randall didn't respond back about the feud to the preacher. The preacher said, "Randall whatever you're going through in 100 years it really won't matter." Little did the preacher know 148 years later it would matter. It would have been nice if Randall and Sarah gave their account, their side of the story, or as the McCoy's call it, "The Truth." It would have cleared up or even prevented a lot of myths over the years. But everyone knows they never talked publically about the feud or took pictures promoting it, other than to the immediate family they never talked at all.

Speak in Anger

When a reporter asked Randall McCoy what he thought about the guys who burnt down his cabin and killed two more of his children. Randall simply told the reporter he had nothing to say. "That God would deal with them." Devil Anse had just orchestrated a massacre and two more of Randall's children had been murdered. Devil Anse had not even been arrested for the three murders he had committed some five years earlier. Now two more of his children are dead. Sure Randall would have liked to have told his side, but he was waiting for the trial, the trail that would never come. This saying always reminds me of Randall McCoy. "Speak in anger and you'll give the best speech you'll ever regret."

If You Lay With Dogs you're going to Get Fleas

Being a Police officer for over thirty years you learn a little bit about people. There's an old saying "If you want to know about someone's character just look at their friends." That speaks volumes for Devil Anse Hatfield. He ran with the same outlaw gang even after the war had ended. It wasn't a matter of home front security. It was more like the "bully brigade." They were the best at it. In fact, in today's culture and times we would refer to them as a gang of thugs up to no good.

Devil Anse Tells True Story
Really?
It was a story alright!

November 1889, Devil Anse was summoned to Charleston, West Virginia to give his deposition or statement concerning the feud. After giving his statement the court reporter read it back to Devil Anse, and he put his mark an "X" on it to authenticate that it was his story. Devil Anse signed his name with an "X" quite frequently as he could not read or write.

I am not going to go into depth on Devil Anse's statement, but it appears as always he knowingly told several lies. We will only insert one or two statements that he swore to under oath. You decide for yourself if he was lying.

Devil Anse stated soon after the pig trial Sam and Paris McCoy way laid Bill Statton and killed him. In fact, it was over two years after the Trial when Bill Staton ambushed Parris and shot him in the back.

Sam McCoy did in fact, kill Bill Staton, and it was ruled self-defense. Devil Anse knew this statement was completely false when he gave it to the courts. Secondly, Devil Anse stated under oath that his son Johnson and Roseanna McCoy a daughter of Randall McCoy ran away and got married. Then a few years later Roseanna had deserted Johnse and is now living with Bad Frank Phillips in Kentucky. Devil Anse knew Roseanna and Johnse never got married. Johnse married Nancy McCoy and had two children they were married for over two years. Devil Anse wanting to discredit the McCoys, fabricated these stories. This is the report the Governor of West Virginia also received.

These two statements along were totally untrue and sworn to by Devil Anse. To be more direct it was straight-out perjury. Devil Anse had known the statements he was giving were untrue. What would telling a lie mean to a man that killed people with no remorse than whipping a dog?

Wheeling Intelligencer
February 4, 1888

THE HATFIELDS-MCCOY FEUD.

Mr. Howell Replies Vigorously to the "Register's" Editorial.

." In my humble way, Mr. Editor, I have done the very best in my power to give the truth in regard to the murder, pillaging and arson that has characterized the conduct of the Hatfield clan, and am willing to await the arbitrament of official history in the matter. **There are two things, however, that must not be lost sight of in this matter, justice to the McCoys and to the State of West Virginia. Not one of the Hatfield gang, not even one of the nine murderers now in jail in Pike County, could be found on the occasion of my visit, to justify the murder of a single McCoy. That five of the McCoy family have been killed under circumstances that have few parallels in criminal history there is no question. Why then have not these murderers been punished?** Simply and solely because Governor Wilson has baffled the efforts of Governor Buckner, of Kentucky, for their apprehension. He has had the requisitions for their apprehension and extradition since September last. Repeated demands have failed to stimulate him to action in the matter. It were better, in his opinion, to allow the State to bear the burden of shame that she is bearing, than to alienate from himself the support of one county solidly Democratic.

It was an act of justice both to the McCoys and Hatfields to determine in a court of justice upon whom the responsibility for these infamous crimes should rest. The solution of it is in the hands of Governor Wilson.

I have no disposition to embargo the progress of West Virginia. I have done as much in my humble way to advance her material interests as any other of her natives. It is not apparent to me, however, how the coddling of a gang of murderers, incendiaries and thieves by the chief magistrate of a State will do anything toward fostering present interests or encouraging valuable immigration. West Virginia needs developing agencies. Capital, energy, enterprise, are all essential to her development. Is the fate of the merchant Glenn any inducement for men of capital to come into West Virginia? In this instance a man of means and energy had gone so far as to marry one of the Hatfield blood, but it availed him nothing, as he was shot at the very feet of his wife, whom his supposed murderer made haste to marry himself.

What West Virginia needs is a Governor who will do all in his power to rid her of such men as the Hatfields (even if he should jeopardize his Senatorial prospects in the effort). Expel the Hatfields; relegate to obscurity the demagogue who sustains and encourages them; make murder a crime and punish the murderer; make the State safe as a habitation for respectable people, and the growth of West Virginia will not be problematical.

Chas. S. Howell.
Pittsburgh, Pa., Feb. 3, 1888.

Courtesy of: West Virginia Archives and History
http://www.wvculture.org/history/hatfieldmccoyarticles.html

The Gangs and Their Differences.

There is a gang in West Virginia banded together for the purpose of murder and rapine. There is a gang in Kentucky whose cohesive principle is the protection of families and homes of men and women. An unresisting family has been deprived of five of its members, a father and mother of five of their children, their homes burned, their effects sent up in smoke, their little substance scattered to the wind, themselves forced out at midnight as wanderers on the bleak and inhospitable mountain side, almost naked in the blasts of winter. A mother stands by and sees her son killed before her very eyes without being allowed to speak to him. Farms are destroyed, religious meetings are broken up, men and women whipped. State and county elections interfered with and terror holds complete sway. To repress the gang that has committed all these crimes was the Kentucky gang organized. These are the gangs, their respective histories, objects and achievements.

I have set forth nothing but what I have obtained by careful investigation, extenuated nothing, magnified nothing. I am confident that everything in the matter of statement of fact and incident is correct. I have talked with scores, adherents of both sides, and have given the substance of their statements. Many refused to allow the use of their names, fearing the venge[a]nce of the Hatfields.

Charles S. Howell.

Courtesy of:West Virginia Archives and History http://www.wvculture.org/history/hatfieldmccoyarticles.htmlCharles S, Howell reporter that investigated the feud. No need for us to comment his reports speak for itself.

Test Your Knowledge

Test Your Knowledge

1. When did the Feud begin?
2. What was Randall McCoy's nickname?
3. Where was Randall McCoy born?
4. When was Anse Hatfield born?
5. What was the name of Randall McCoy's Parents?
6. What was the name of Randall's wife?
7. What was the name of Devil Anse's parents?
8. What was the name of the river that separated Devil Anse and Randall McCoy?

9. How many children did Randall McCoy have?
10. What was Anse Hatfield's nickname?
11. Who was Randall McCoy's favorite child?
12. When was Randall McCoy born?
13. What was Devil Anse's wife name?
14. How many children did Devil Anse have?
15. Devil Anse had how many brothers and sister?
16. How many brother's and sister's did Randall have?
17. Who was Cottontop's dad?
18. How long did the Feud last?
19. Who was the first death connected with the feud?
20. Devil Anse was the leader of what gang?
21. Which side did Asa Harmon McCoy fight on?
22. Why was Harmon McCoy discharged early?
23. When Asa Harmon returned home where did he live (hide out) before his death?

24. Who was the only person to be charged and hung during the feud?
25. Who were the two that fell in love?
26. When did Johnse and Roseanna meet?
27. What was the name of Roseanna & Johnse baby?
28. What were the children spanked with?
29. Who was known as a deserter?
30. Who was known as one of the most beautiful girls in Pike County?
31. What kind of business did Devil Anse have?
32. What was stolen from Randall McCoy?
33. Who stole it?
34. How many Hatfield's and McCoy's where on the jury?
35. Who went against Randall during the trail?
36. What are the two main ways that people during this time supported themselves in Appalachia?
37. How many acres did Randall McCoy own?
38. What are two sayings that still are said

Today?
39. Which Hatfield was hurt during cutting down trees?
40. What was the name of Rosanna's cousin who married Johnse?
41. Who did the Ky. Governor appoint Deputy Sheriff to bring the Hatfield's to justice?
42. Who was Nancy McCoy's brother that Jim Vance and Cap Hatfield killed?
43. When was Devil Anse's brother killed?
44. What kind of trees where the three McCoy boys tied to?
45. The three boys bodies where described as what?
46. When did the feud reach its peak?
47. Who was Devil Anse's Uncle?
48. Where was Roseanna and Johnse baby buried?
49. How old was the baby?
50. What was Johnse's nickname?
51. What did the winning team receive as a prize in 1979 on the game show family

feud with the Hatfield's and McCoy's?

52. Who did Nancy McCoy marry after her brother was killed?
53. How old was Devil Anse when he died?
54. In what year did Randall McCoy die?
55. What year did Devil Anse die?
56. How old was Randall McCoy when he died?
57. What was the investigators name that the Governor sent to Pike County?
58. Who was the Governor of West Virginia at the time of the Feud?
59. Who was the Governor of Kentucky at the time of the Feud?
60. Who killed Bad Frank Phillips?
61. What was the name of Jim Vance's dog?
62. What year did the Feud end?
63. How many of Randall McCoy children died during the Feud?
64. How old was Roseanna when she died?
65. Who were the three boys tied to Paw Paw trees?
66. How did Devil Anse get his nickname?

67. What is bushwacked?
68. On which side of the Tug River where the McCoy boys killed on?
69. What was the name of the two children killed during the Cabin Massacre?
70. In the end who won the Feud?

Answers

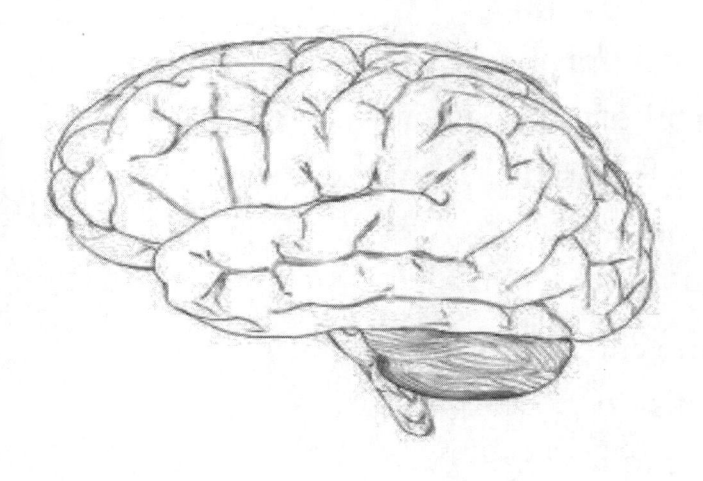

1. 1864
2. Ole Ran'l
3. Pike County, Kentucky
4. September 9, 1839
5. Daniel & Margaret McCoy
6. Sarah "Sally" McCoy
7. Ephraim & Nancy Hatfield
8. Tug River
9. 16
10. Devil Anse
11. Roseanna
12. October 30, 1825

13. Levicey Chafin Hatfield
14. 13
15. 17 brothers and Sisters
16. 12 brothers and Sisters
17. Ellison Hatfield
18. 27 years
19. Asa Harmon McCoy
20. Logan Wildcats
21. Union side
22. He broke his leg
23. Blue Springs
24. Cottontop
25. Roseanna McCoy & Johnse Hatfield
26. Election Day in 1880 (Kentucky polling place Blackberry Creek
27. Little Sarah Elizabeth
28. Cow tails
29. Devil Anse Hatfield
30. Roseanna McCoy
31. Timber
32. Razor back pig
33. Floyd Hatfield
34. 6 Hatfield and 6 McCoy
35. Selkerk McCoy and Bill Staton

36. Farming & Hunting
37. 300 acres
38. Real McCoy and What in the Sam hill
39. William Cap Hatfield
40. Nancy McCoy
41. Bad Frank Phillips
42. Jefferson McCoy
43. 1882 during the election
44. Paw paw
45. Bullet Riddled
46. When Devil Anse and Jim Vance set Randall McCoy's house on fire then shot his family when they came out. (New Year's Eve.)
47. Jim Vance
48. Burnwell (Aflex Kentucky)
49. 8 months old
50. Lover Boy
51. A pig
52. Bad Frank Phillips
53. 82 years old
54. March 28, 1914
55. January 6, 1921
56. 88 years old

57. Sam Hill
58. E. Willis Wilson
59. S. B. Buckner
60. Ransom Bray
61. Miles Jr.
62. 1891
63. He lost 7 of his children (5 murdered) Roseanna and William died of natural causes
64. 29 years old
65. Tolbert, Phamer and Randall Jr.
66. When he was six years old his mother said, "Anse you're meaner than the Devil.
67. Ambushed
68. Kentucky side.
69. Calvin and Alifair
70. No one

Receipt for a feud

Two Stubborn men

Too much pride

Too much moonshine

Too many sons

Too many guns

Too little sense

Accumulation of problems and disagreements that exist between the two families

Throw it all into a pot then stir it up for a little while until it begins to boil.

Those are the ingredients for a Feud.

Timeline

1863

- Devil Anse Hatfield desserts Confederate Army and forms guerrilla band. Raids and thefts follow from the Logan Widcats.

1865

- First death in feud -- Asa Harmon McCoy. Devil Anse or his Logan Wildcats-No prosecution.
- Civil War ends in May.
- President Lincoln shot by John Wilkes Booth (Apr 4).
- Thirteenth Amendment, abolishing slavery takes effect (Dec 18).

1875

- The Kentucky Derby is held at Churchill Downs Louisville, Ky. for the first time (May 17).

1878

- Randolph McCoy finds out Floyd Hatfield has stolen his pig.
- Bill Staton's lying testimony in court later wins trial for Floyd Hatfield.

1880

- Bill Staton shoots Parris McCoy in the back. Is then killed by Sam McCoy.
- Sam McCoy tried in September for Bill Staton's Death. He is acquitted **(Not Guilty)** Ruled Self-Defense.

1881

- Roseanna McCoy and Johnse Hatfield meet.
- Johnse is captured by McCoy boys. Roseanna's ride to Devil Anse's saves Johnse's life.
- Hatfield's burn Asa McCoy's Cabin to the ground

1882

- Roseanna returns home and then moves to Uriah and Betty McCoy's her aunt and uncles to have baby.

- Ellison Hatfield is fatally wounded by Pharmer McCoy on August 9th
- Devil Anse ties Tolbert, Pharmer and Randall Jr. to three trees and they are executed.

1886

- Jeff McCoy (son of Asa Harmon McCoy) is killed on banks of the Tug.

1887

- Kentucky governor appoints Bad Frank Phillips as Deputy Sheriff to capture Devil Anse, Jim Vance and the others for the kidnapping and murderers of the McCoy boys.

1888

- In an attempt to kill all witnesses against Devil Anse and his gang he plans a New Year's Eve attack on Ole Ran'l McCoy's cabin.
- Leaves Alifair and Calvin dead,

  Randalls wife Sarah beat and left for dead as well as his home burned to the ground.

1889

- Roseanna McCoy, less than 30 years old, dies in Pikeville

- The murder trial of some of the Hatfield clan for the murdering of the three McCoy boys' begins.

1890

- Ellison "Cottontop" Mounts is executed for the murder of Alifair McCoy. (Feb 18).

1891
The Feud ends.

Randall and Sarah's Children

Randolph McCoy married Sarah "Sally" McCoy (born 1829; died in the 1890s), daughter of Samuel McCoy and Elizabeth Davis, on December 9, 1849 in Pike County, Kentucky. They had 16 children together. Their children were as follows:

- Josephine McCoy, daughter (1848 –)
- James H. "Uncle Jim" McCoy, son (1849 – 1929)
- Floyd McCoy, son (1853 – 1928)
- Tolbert McCoy, son (1854 – 1882)
- Lilburn McCoy, son (1855 –)
- Samuel McCoy, son (1856 – 1921)
- unnamed infant daughter (1857 – 1857)
- Alifair McCoy, daughter (1858 – 1888)
- Roseanna McCoy, daughter (1859 – 1888)
- Calvin McCoy, son (1862 – 1888)
- Pharmer McCoy, son (1863 – 1882)
- Randolph "Bud" McCoy, son (1864 – 1882)
- William McCoy, son (1866 –)
- Trinvilla "Trinnie" McCoy, daughter (1868 –)
- Adelaide McCoy, daughter (1870 –)
- Fannie McCoy, daughter (1873 – 1943)

Devil Anse and Levisa Hatfield's Children

William Anderson "Devil Anse" Hatfield married Levisa "Levicy" Chafin (December 20, 1842 – March 15, 1929), the daughter of Nathaniel Chafin and Matilda Varney, on April 18, 1861 in Logan County, West Virginia (then Virginia). Their 13 children were as follows:

- Johnson "Johnse" Hatfield (1862 – 1922)
- William Anderson "Cap" Hatfield (1864 – 1930)
- Robert E. Lee "Bob" Hatfield (1866 – 1931)
- Nancy Arvella "Belle"/"Nannie" Hatfield Vance Mullins (1869 – 1939)
- Elliott Rutherford Hatfield (1872 – 1932)
- Mary Hatfield Hensley Simpkins Howes (1874 – 1963)
- Elizabeth "Betty" Hatfield Caldwell (1876 – 1962)
- Elias M. Hatfield (1878 – 1911)
- Detroit W. "Troy" Hatfield (1881 – 1911)
- Joseph Davis Hatfield (1883 – 1963)
- Rose Lee "Rosie" Hatfield Browning (1885 – 1965)
- Emmanuel Wilson "Willis" Hatfield (1888 – 1978)
- Tennyson Samuel "Tennis" Hatfield (1890 – 1953)

Hatfield and McCoy Friends.

I grew up on Blackberry Creek only a little ways up the road from where the pig trial and the election fight were held. Furthermore, just up the road from Paul Hatfield who has been my best friend since childhood. Paul and I grew up and went to school together. During the 1980s we both worked for the Pike County Sheriff's Department. This was the same Sheriff's Dept. that Frank Phillips, Tolbert and Jim McCoy worked for in the 1880s some 100 years earlier.

My brother Barry was our K-9 Officer, Paul and I served as Deputy Sheriff's Special Investigators as well as Detectives. Paul was our Supervisor in charge of the Belfry Branch of the Sheriff's Dept. Belfry is just a few miles from the West Virginia border, as well as Randall McCoy's original home place. The location where his cabin was burnt and two of his children were murdered. Just across Blackberry mountain was the location of the Pig Trail and Election ground.

Paul and I excelled in undercover drug investigations and made hundreds of Drug Raids and Arrest. Being a Hatfield and McCoy working together was always interesting. We would go to other states to pick up prisoners or on investigations. We would identify ourselves and show our badges only to be looked at in the weirdest manner. The officer's from the other departments just couldn't believe our real names were Hatfield and McCoy, and that we were from Kentucky the home of the feud. It would really blow their minds when we would tell them that it was actually our ancestor in the feud. Needless to say we went through a lot of business cards.

As I sit here typing and reminiscing about my friend, I think of so many memories. We've been in some tight spots together in them old hills of Eastern Kentucky. No better partner or friend and no other back-up needed once Paul Hatfield arrived on the scene. Too bad Devil Anse and Randall didn't have the friendship we have had.

Detective, Fred McCoy, K-9 Officer, Barry McCoy, Detective, Paul Hatfield

Confederate Soldiers

Virginia State Line/45th Infantry Battalion

Over the years, we have read where someone has said they could find no record of Randall McCoy ever serving in the Confederate Army with Devil Anse. We have also read in some Hatfield and McCoy books where the author stated, Randall fought on the side of the North, and Devil Anse had fought for the South. These statements have been printed in books, and both are incorrect. Some authors just throw a book together and think as long as it has Hatfield and McCoy in the title then it will sell. Of course, they are correct, when it comes to collectors of Hatfield and McCoy memorabilia. That's been the problem over the years they just throw a book together without regards to the truth.

So to set the record straight it is a fact that Randall McCoy along with My GG Grandfather Uriah McCoy fought for the Confederate Army. They both served with the Virginia State Line and then with the 45th Infantry Battalion, which is the same Battalion that Devil Anse Hatfield, Ellison Hatfield and several more solders from the Tug Valley area deserted from on or about Dec. 19th 1863. Both Randall and his brother in law Uriah McCoy was asked by Devil Anse to return home with the rest of the soldiers who were deserting at that time. Both refused to leave their fellow soldiers and continued to serve until the war ended in 1865.

Randall to be Victimized Again

I recently saw in the newspaper where donations were being accepted in order to buy a monument to honor Randall McCoy. The proposed monument would have Randall with his arms crossed as in disgust of Roseanna who is standing opposite of Randall and holding her baby. In between the two is Sarah McCoy holding her Bible which from all accounts would have been an accurate description of her. As for Randall's arms being crossed to depict him being mad or pouting at Roseanna this is an insult.

Why not have Randall looking at the grave site where six of his children are buried, five of them killed by assassination. Or at the grave of his brother and nephew who were also assassinated. There was so much more to the feud then Roseanna's love affair or the pig. It was about the death of their children. Over the years everyone has seemed to forget these two parents lost seven children during this feud five of them so violently it's almost to unimaginable to uncomprehend.

Someone's watching too much of the History Channels mini soap opera. As was stated earlier don't believe everything you see on television.

Contrary to fiction Randall and Roseanna mended their relationship. After Sarah was brutally beaten, Roseanna moved to Pikeville to care for both her mom and dad who were well into their sixties by then. Rosanna continued to live with Sarah and Randall until the age of 29 when she died of pneumonia. Her father Randall buried her next to where he and Sarah would eventually be entombed. Does this sound to you like someone who despises their child? Out of sixteen of Randall's children he chose Roseanna to be buried next to him and Sarah. Remember Randall out lived both Sarah and Roseanna. He alone chose their location to be buried. It's common sense; people can continue to believe the myths and un-truths that have been told over the years or look at the clues, better yet the facts for a better understanding.

We hope they reconsider the monument for Randall with a more suitable one showing the restraint he had shown by not escalating the feud and taking justice into his own hands. Also showing the grief Randall had from the loss of his children.

My wife Shelia along with my brother Barry McCoy and I came up with this one.

Randall and Sarah holding hands, Sarah holding her Bible, overlooking a duplicate tombstone of their six children buried at Hardy. Just off to the side is Roseanna kneeling at the headstone of Sarah Elizabeth. Her hands over her face grieving for the loss of her baby daughter.

The Randolph McCoy Family - Sketch Courtesy of Shelia McCoy

This would serve three purposes, one a monument for Randall and Sarah McCoy. Secondly, a duplicate tombstone for the six children buried on the Vance property at Hardy that no one is allowed to visit except family. Third, a monument for Roseanna with a duplicate head stone of her baby's grave at Stringtown. The grave is so high on the hill we hear a lot of older people say they can't make the climb up the stairs to see it.

Starving for Attention

(They say a picture is worth a thousand words)

It seems that if there was a camera around Devil Anse was going to be in its lens. Remember, this is the mid to late 1800's, photo equipment and film was not cheap, nor was it easy to locate. However, Devil Anse always seemed to find it. Above you have his children and even grandchildren displaying guns for a family photo.

This picture was said to have been taken after the New Year's Eve Massacre. He's posing for the newspaper reporters with his family while Randall and Sarah are burying two more of their children. Wait! Let us re-phase that, While Randall was burying two more of their children. Sarah had been beaten so badly she was unable to attend Calvin and

Alifairs funeral. The pictures are too numerous to count that Devil Anse posed for during the feud. Let us not take the word "Feud" lightly "during the time Devil Anse and his gang was killing Randall and Sarah's children".

As was stated before he was without a doubt a hedonist. Some say Devil Anse was a smart businessman. Others say he got his start from robbing and stealing when he was the leader of the Wildcats. It's not really that hard to get a good start in life when you just take it from others.

Devil Anse loved the recognition and attention he received from the news media during the feud. Seems he and his grandson Cottontop had more in common than most people realized. He must have had an IQ even less then Cottontop to not have realized he was getting all that attention from doing the unthinkable, MURDERING children and young adults.

As you continue to read other books and research the Hatfield and McCoy Feud keep in mind Devil Anse Hatfield was a "Bad Man" who did some horrible things during his lifetime. Over the years Devil Anse Hatfield's family has relished being in the spotlight with all the attention the name has brought them. The wild scraggly beard, the tall tales he told to anyone who would listen, even down to the dirty deeds and atrocities he brought not only to the McCoys but many others in the Tug Valley area during his life. Don't be fooled by the title on his monument or the books that have been written over the years wanting to make Devil Anse Hatfield bigger than life.

Just as Randall McCoy failed to tell his side back in the days of the mayhem so have his McCoy descendants. As of the writing of this book that has ceased. We hope that anyone who reads this book remembers two things. One, there was no winners during the feud and secondly, Devil Anse Hatfield was nothing more than a modern day terrorist and murderer. You can place a monument over a murderer, but in the end he's still a murderer.

(Devil Anse) Hatfield sat for this portrait in 1911. He was then 74 years old, rich, famous and still held unaccountable for many murders. He paid Artist Henry Craven $75 for the picture.(according to Life Magazine May 22nd 1944)

In Closing

Randall McCoy was a man who lost many members of his family to a murderer. A murderer, who was never brought to Justice or held accountable for his actions.

I can't imagine losing one child. It is inconceivable losing five children and especially when the same man is responsible for all their deaths. This wasn't about pride this was a man who did the right thing. He lived by the law of the land. He was not the villain here.

It was said Randall had a Dance with the Devil. It wasn't a dance it was a nightmare not only for Randall but for his entire family. Talk about a case of being bullied. Over the years, it seems that everyone has been afraid to say anything negative about Devil Anse.

No one has to favor one side or the other. Just tell the truth and let the chips fall where they may. Investigate the Feud like the crime that it was. Randall McCoy was a victim, he never killed anyone. Devil Anse was a murderer. A monument is put up, and he becomes a hero.

Randall was a father, Christian and husband. The fact is that even more could have been killed during the feud had Randall not chose to trust in the Justice System. (Even-though it failed him in the end.)

After the cabin massacre family and friends came out in droves to support Randall. They were outraged. Not once did Randall say, "let's kill them all." This is the very reason why our ancestors should have talked through the years. Some say silence is golden, but, it's a two edge sword. Silence can also be Damming. This is a good example of Good vs Bad and the bad winning. I hope they are all in Heaven today.

However, let's not overlook Devil Anse's atrocities during the feud. Let's forgive but not forget. What kind of example does this send to our children and grandchildren? Do what you want, kill, steal, cheat and lie. If the law gets charges and indictments on you, just hideout. Then when you die have a huge monument put up, and no one will even look at how you lived your life. They will just assume you must have been a good person. Maybe, even a hero.

Cap, Johnse, Wall and others went to court then to prison and did their time. Jim and Cottontop were killed. It just seems like Devil Ance would have had to have gone through the same process as his sons. If a father instigated a crime, and his sons followed his lead and went to prison seems like the father would have felt guilty and remorseful. If not for the crime itself at least for using bad judgment, and causing his sons to be incarcerated.

If Tolbert and Pharmer had not been executed, they should have gone to jail for what they did to Ellison. Since Devil Anse did to the McCoy boys what they did to Ellison, he should have been held responsible. If you don't agree with that then you're not being fair. If, you do agree, then Devil Anse got away with murder. I read once where one of the Hatfields said that Devil Anse's family had fared better than Randall's.

There is more to life than a bank account. Randall once said, "If you want to know how rich you are, add up all the things that money can't buy." Devil Anse seemed always to be in a conflict with someone. A lot of his children followed his lead several were even killed, with no connection to the McCoy's or the feud but during other squabbles. Many of them dealt in the sale of untaxed and illegal alcohol (moonshine) Randall may have figured if he had to get rich illegally he didn't want it. To some people in life morals mean more than money or property.

Credentials

Fred McCoy was born and raised in the Tug Valley area. He grew up on Blackberry Creek, in Pike County. Just up the road from where the famous Pig Trial, Election Day Fight and the location where the three McCoy boys were assassinated. He joined the U.S. Marine Corps in 1975 at the age of 17. After serving three years in the Marines he attended Florida Junior College in Jacksonville, Florida and worked as an auxiliary Deputy Sheriff with the Jacksonville Sheriff's Dept. from Nov 1978-March 1980. Upon returning home to Pike County, Kentucky Fred attended Eastern Kentucky University and Kentucky Department of Criminal Justice Training he worked for the Pike County Sheriff's Dept. until 1989, a year later he took a job as Chief of Police with a small central Kentucky town. Over his extensive Law Enforcement career of approximately thirty three years Fred has served in just about every capacity from Deputy Sheriff, Special Investigator, Detective, to Chief of Police. Fred received the Firearms award from both Florida and Kentucky Police Academies for shooting high score. Over the years he has completed or been certified in many areas of Law Enforcement including: Accident Investigation, Breath Test Operator, Police Firearms Instructor, C.C.D.W. Instructor/Trainer, Certified Taser X26, Certified in Rapid Deployment (Dealing with active shooters in schools, etc.) "Street Survival by West Virginia Troopers Association, "Drug Interdiction by the University of Delaware, Firearms Decision Making, Domestic Violence, Crime Scene Investigations, Orientation for new Police Chiefs, Child Abuse Investigations, Robbery Investigations, Police Executive Command, Hostage and Crisis Negotiator, Patrol Handgun, Advanced Latent Prints, Homeland Security, Prescription Drug Abuse Investigations, Stress Management, Ethics, Background Investigations, Hazardous Material Symposium, Methamphetamine update and many more. Over the years Fred has received many awards and citations including the Police Medal of Honor, Medal of Valor, and Outstanding Investigation among many others. He is a Certified Police Firearms Instructor last twenty-eight years, Certified CCDW instructor last seventeen years, also a Certified CCDW Instructor Trainer which means he's certified to train others as CCDW Instructors. Shelia McCoy is also a State Certified CCDW Instructor and has taught or assisted in the Certification of thousands of Kentuckians with obtaining their Kentucky Gun Permits.

The McCoy's

My Grandmother and Grandfather Ella Jane McCoy and Phillip McCoy (standing center) My Dad "Bobby Bryant McCoy" (kneeling in front)

Phillip McCoy, born 27 February 1890, Married **Ella Jane Smith**, who were the parents of:

Mabel McCoy, who married Jonah Hatfield, **Myrel McCoy,** who married 1st Monroe Dotson: 2nd Bob Sullivan. **Dayrl McCoy**, who married Floyd Hatfield, brother to Jonah. **Dolly McCoy,** who Married Ancy Dotson, brother to Monroe. **Asa McCoy**, who married Elsie Mayhorn. **Grace McCoy**, who married Ransom Hager. **Agnes McCoy**, who married Lawson Hager. **Lorene McCoy**, who married Delmer Ally. **Lucas McCoy**, who married Ruby Oliver. *** Bobby Bryant McCoy** who married *Coralea Morley   *My Dad and Mom

As of 2010, the population was 65,024. Its county seat is Pikeville. Pike is Kentucky's largest county in terms of land area. Pike County is the 11th largest county in Kentucky in terms of population. Pike County was founded on December 19, 1821. The county was named for General Zebulon Pike, the explorer who discovered Pikes Peak. Between 1860 and 1891 the Hatfield-McCoy feud raged in Pike and in bordering Mingo County, West Virginia. On May 6, 1893, Pikeville officially became a city and the county seat. Pike County is also home to Paul E. Patton, former governor of Kentucky

My Great-Great Grandfather, Uriah McCoy's Grave Stone

Coordinates: 37 37.802 N 82 13.215 W

URIAH MCCOY
1824 — 1889
SON OF SAMUEL MCCOY
GRANDSON OF WILLIAM MCCOY

BETTY ELIZABETH
RUTHERFORD MCCOY
1826 — 1915
DAUGHTER OF RUBEN RUTHERFORD

This is my GG Grandparents where Roseanna went to live and have her baby. This is the aunt Betty that Roseanna was so close to. Uriah McCoy My Great Great Grandfather and Sarah McCoy, Randall's wife were brother and sister. Roseanna even named her baby Sarah Elizabeth after both her mother and her aunt Betty.

Asa McCoy son of Uriah McCoy was my Great Grandfather
1854-1922

(married Nancy Hatfield on Sept. 23rd 1875) she was "Preacher" Anderson Hatfield's daughter.

Phillip and Ella McCoy 1954

My Grandfather and Grandmother

Phillip and Ella Jane McCoy

My Grandparents Phillip and Ella Jane McCoy's Grave

Dotson Cemetery

Blackberry, Kentucky

Same cemetery the lower half is the Dotson Cemetery the upper part from the holly bush to the top of the mountain is the Bobby McCoy Memorial Cemetery

My Parents

Bobby and Cora Lea (Morley) McCoy

My Dad and Moms Grave site

Bobby McCoy Memorial Cemetery

Blackberry, Kentucky

Same cemetery the lower half is the Dotson Cemetery the upper part from the holly bush to the top of the mountain is the Bobby McCoy Memorial Cemetery

SITE OF RANDOLPH McCOY HOUSE

House was located on Blackberry Fork of Pond Creek. It burned Jan. 1, 1888, during a Hatfield raid. Two of Randolph's children, Alifair and Calvin, were killed in attack; their mother Sally was badly injured. Randolph and other children escaped. Site is part of Hatfield-McCoy Feud Historic Dist.
Presented by Pikeville-Pike County Tourism

Coordinates: 37° 36.196' N, 82° 12.85' W. Marker is near Hardy, Kentucky, in Pike County

Baby's Grave Site

Sarah Elizabeth "Little Sally" was the daughter of Roseanna McCoy and Johnse Hatfield. She was born in the spring of 1881 and died when she was only eight months old. In 1880 Roseanna met Johnse at an Election Day celebration on Blackberry Creek, in Pike County Kentucky. They slipped away from the crowd and when they returned the polling place was deserted. Fearful of her family's reaction Roseanna went home with Johnse to West Virginia. Devil Anse would not allow his son to wed the daughter of Randolph McCoy. Roseanna loved Johnse and stayed with him in Devil Anse's home but became discouraged because he was unfaithful. Disillusioned, she returned home to Kentucky to have Johnse's baby. Her father rejected her and Roseanna went to live with her Aunt Betty at Stringtown, Kentucky. Sarah Elizabeth is buried on the hilltop under the pine trees above the Uriah McCoy house. Broken-hearted after the baby's death, Roseanna grieved at the grave and lost her will to live.

Coordinates: 37 37.802 N 82 13.215 W

My Beautiful wife and Co Author Shelia McCoy in front of Randall McCoy's well at Hardy, Kentucky the original site of Randall and Sarah's Cabin before it was burnt to the ground in 1888. This is the well Alifair was going to fetch water from when she was murdered by the Hatfields. Same area where Calvin was murdered in the New Year's Massacre.

Coordinates: 37 36.182N 82 12.915W

FRANK AND NANCY
PHILLIPS
CEMETERY

IN MEMORY OF
FRANK PHILIPS
BORN
Jul. 27. 1861
DIED
Jul. 12. 1898

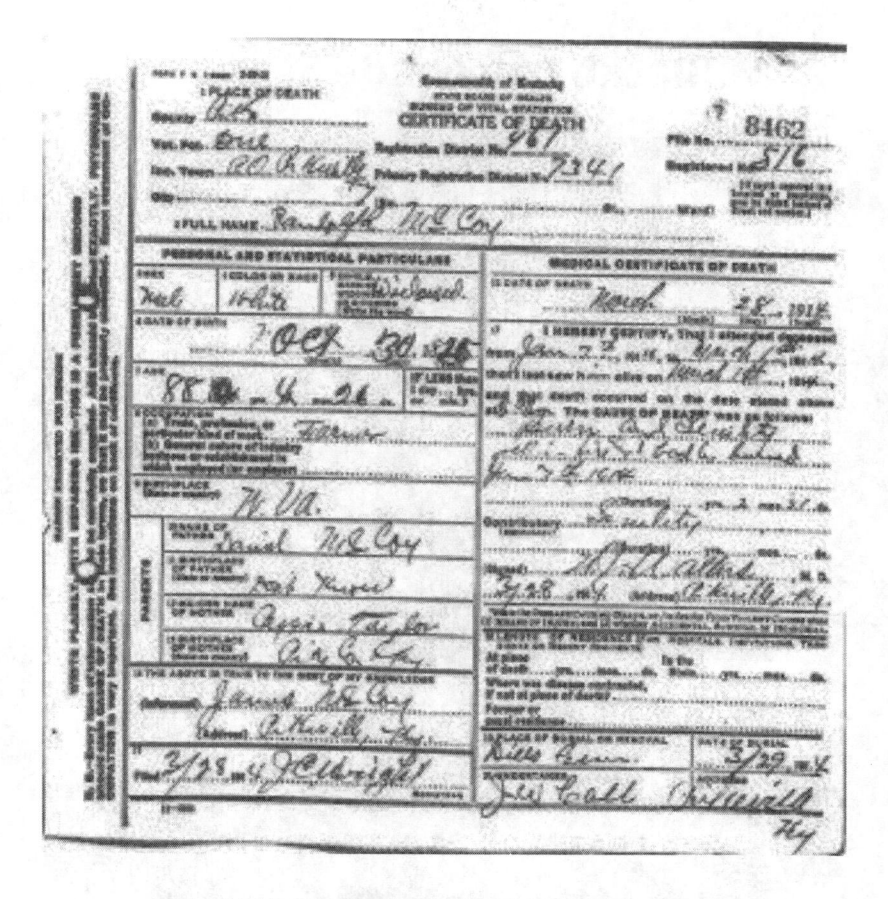

Randall McCoy's Death Certificate

Occupation - Farmer, Cause of Death – Fire, Burns, Marital Status - Widowed, Place of Death - Pike County, Place of Burial - Dils Cemetery, Funeral Home - J.W. Calls

Blackberry Grade School

This is where I attended grade school as a child 1st-8th grade, lot of memories lining up at these two doors after recess each day.

"Preacher" Anderson Hatfield's Cabin where the Pig Trial was held. Also where the election grounds were located in Blackberry, Kentucky. Just to the right of the pic (out of frame) in a field was where the Election Day fight took place. This was also the home place for my Great Grandmother Nancy Hatfield who married my great Grandfather Asa McCoy

Coordinates: 37° 34.814' N, 82° 10.806' W. Marker is in

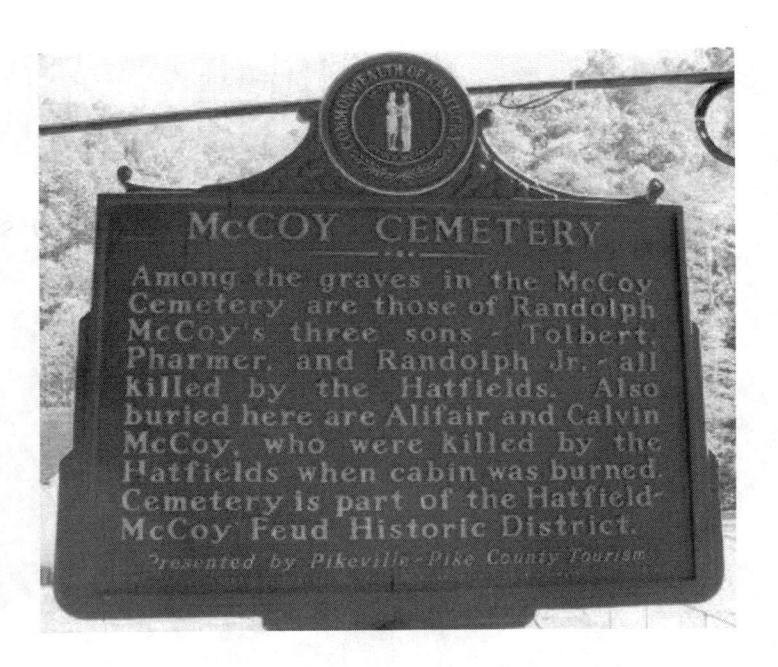

Coordinates: 37° 34.817' N, 82° 10.793' W. Marker is in McCarr, Kentucky, in Pike County.

The grave marker of six of Randall and Sarah's children at Hardy, Kentucky just across from where the Cabin Massacres occurred.

HATFIELD-McCOY FEUD

The feud resulted, in part, from Civil War conflicts, romantic entanglements, family-oriented discord, property and election disputes, mixed with mountain pride. Violence surrounding clan leaders Anderson Hatfield and Randolph McCoy eventually involved governors of Kentucky and West Virginia. Deaths and time brought an end to the feud. See over.

Myself and Shelia at the Dils Cemetery, just below the grave of Randall and Sarah McCoy

Dils Cemetery

THE DILS CEMETERY

The Dils Cemetery is believed to be the first integrated cemetery in Eastern Kentucky. Colonel John Dils, who was opposed to slavery, gave many freed slaves jobs in his tannery and general store. He later provided gravesites for them and their descendants.

While more than one hundred thirty African-American graves have been located in this historic spot, only forty-nine of those have been correctly identified. It is our hope that further investigation will bring to light the remaining names and stories.

The Dils Cemetery research project has been conducted through funds provided by the African-American Heritage Commission and the Pikeville-Pike County Tourism Commission.

Coordinates: 37 deg 28 min 39.005 sec N 82 deg 30 min 52.775 W

Dils Cemetery

Colonel John Dils purchased the property in 1871 on which this cemetery is located. He was the colonel of the 39th Kentucky Infantry in the Civil War. In addition to Colonel Dils, there are several Civil War veterans buried here with the original Union military markers. The cemetery is listed on the National Register of Historic Places as part of the Hatfield-McCoy Feud District and has changed little since 1871. It is the final resting place of several participants in the Hatfield-McCoy Feud. Buried here are Randolph McCoy, the famed leader of the McCoy family, his wife Sarah, their daughter Roseanna, their son Sam and his wife, Martha. The cemetery is the first known racially integrated cemetery in Eastern Kentucky. 130 of the 500 graves, many of them unmarked, are African American.

Randall and Sarah McCoy's grave site located at the Dils Cemetery overlooking the town of Pikeville, Kentucky

Shelia and Fred McCoy standing at Randall and Sarah McCoy's grave site. Randall McCoy and Uriah McCoy, Fred's GG Grandfather's dads were brothers.

Rosanna's grave located right next to her father and mothers grave at Dils Cemetery. This should refute all those who said Randall never talked to his daughter again and disowned her. He himself buried her here and picked out the spot for him and Sarah to be buried next to his daughter.

Sam McCoy (son of Randall) and his wife Martha's grave site just a ways from Randall's grave at the Dils Cemetery in Pikeville, Kentucky.

Historical Marker in front of Randall and Sarah's home in Pikeville, Kentucky. This is where the family moved to after the New Year's Massacre when their cabin was burnt down by the Hatfield's and Crazy Jim Vance

Randall and Sarah's house in Pikeville, Kentucky

Old courthouse:

PIKE CO. COURTHOUSE AND JAIL

Courthouse erected 1888-89 by McDonald Bros.; later renovated 1932-33. Here was scene of Hatfield clan trials for murders of Tolbert, Randolph, Jr., Pharmer, Alifair and Calvin McCoy. The defendants lodged in adjacent jail; found guilty and sentenced to life in prison except Ellison Mounts, hanged February 18, 1890. Courthouse and jail part of Hatfield-McCoy Feud Historic Dist.

Coordinates: 37 deg 28 min 44.991 N 82 deg 31 min 3.445 W

GRAVE OF SALLY McCOY

Sally McCoy contracted measles and pneumonia, and died a few months after her birth. The death of Rosanna McCoy's only child, Sally, was a contributing factor in the grief and sorrow that led to the untimely death of Roseanna. Sally was laid to rest in the cemetery at top of hill. Grave is listed on the National Register of Historic Places.

Sarah "Sally" Elizabeth McCoy was the baby girl of Rosanna and Johnse. She was named after Roseanna's mother (Sarah) and my GG Grandmother (Elizabeth McCoy) (aka Betty) who was my GG Grandfather Uriah McCoy's wife.

SARAH ELIZABETH
1881 ———— 1881
DAUGHTER OF
ROSEANNA McCOY JOHNSE HATFIELD

Randall McCoy's wife Sarah was my GG Grandfather Uriah McCoy's sister. Over the years author and reporters have stated Betty and Sarah were sisters. In all reality they were sister n laws.

This is my GG Grandparents Uriah and Betty McCoy's house Located at Burnwell, Kentucky. It was built in the 1800's. This is where Roseanna went to live and gave birth to her baby girl. Sarah Elizabeth

To the right as you are facing the house on the hill is where Roseanna's baby Sarah Elizabeth is buried.

To the left as you are facing the house on the hill is where my GG Grandparents Uriah and Betty McCoy are buried.

Myself and my wife Shelia standing in front of my GG Grandparents Uriah and Betty McCoy's house located in Burnwell, Kentucky

This is another Roseanna McCoy Monument Located at Blackberry Park on Ky. Hwy 1056 near Blackberry Grade School.

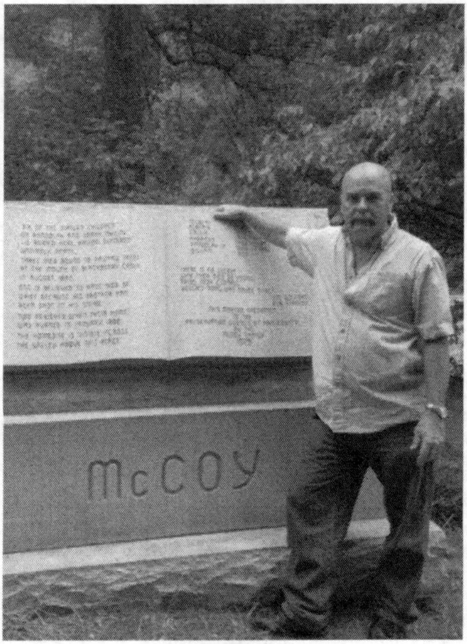
McCOY

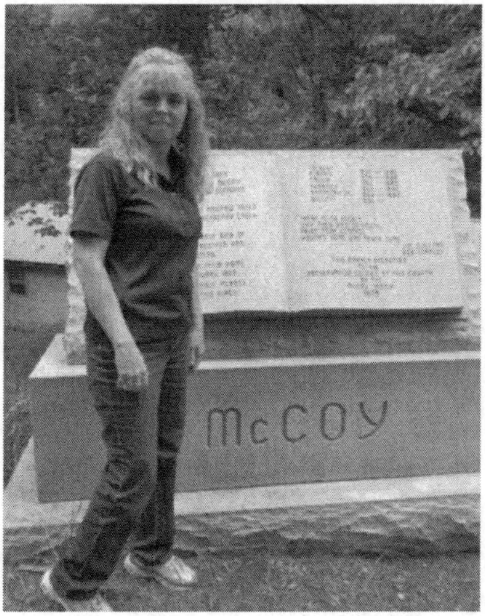
McCOY

Fred McCoy Baptized by a Hatfield

Brother John Calvin Hatfield & Brother Bob Sullivan

Baptizing me at 16 yrs. old

No better man then John Calvin Hatfield "a preacher that practiced what he preached every day of his life not just on Sundays".

Ricky McCoy, Bobby McCoy (Father), and Freddy McCoy approximately 1961 in front of Blackberry Restaurant my mom and dad owned and operated.

My mom and dad when they were kids and as adults

Our son Bobby & Angel (Turpin) McCoy

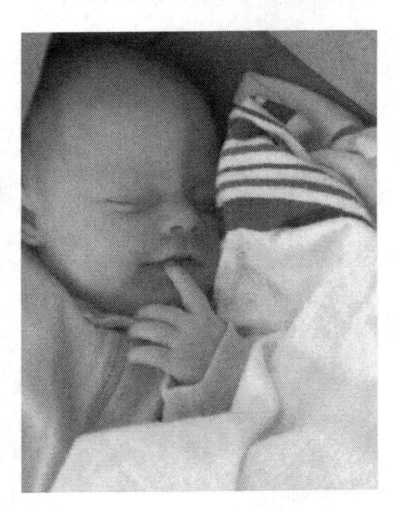

Granddaughter Emily

Jimmy, Ella Jane (McCoy) daughter, and Ethaniel Schuler

Grandson Ethaniel with his dad Jimmy Schuler our Son-In-law

Devil Anse Hatfield Collector Lamps

Sold in sets of two in 1975 first edition only 300 sets made. My dad bought these for my mother when they first came out in 1975

Randall McCoy Collector Lamps

Sold in sets of two in 1975 first edition only 300 sets made.

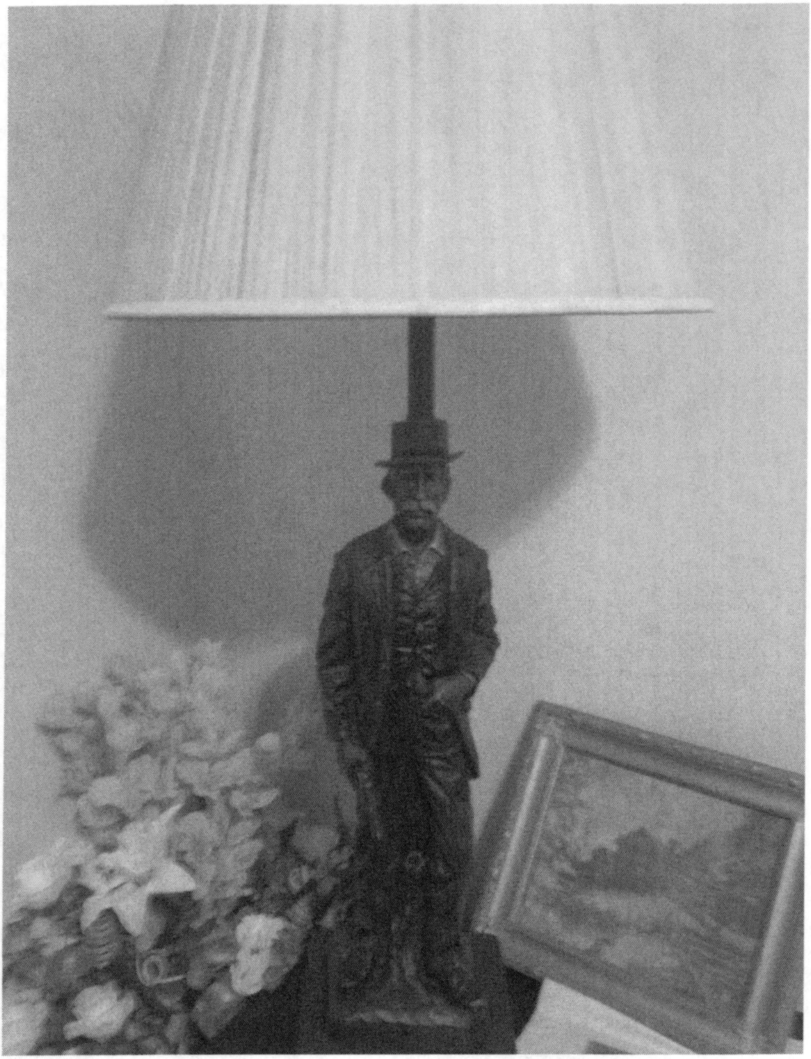

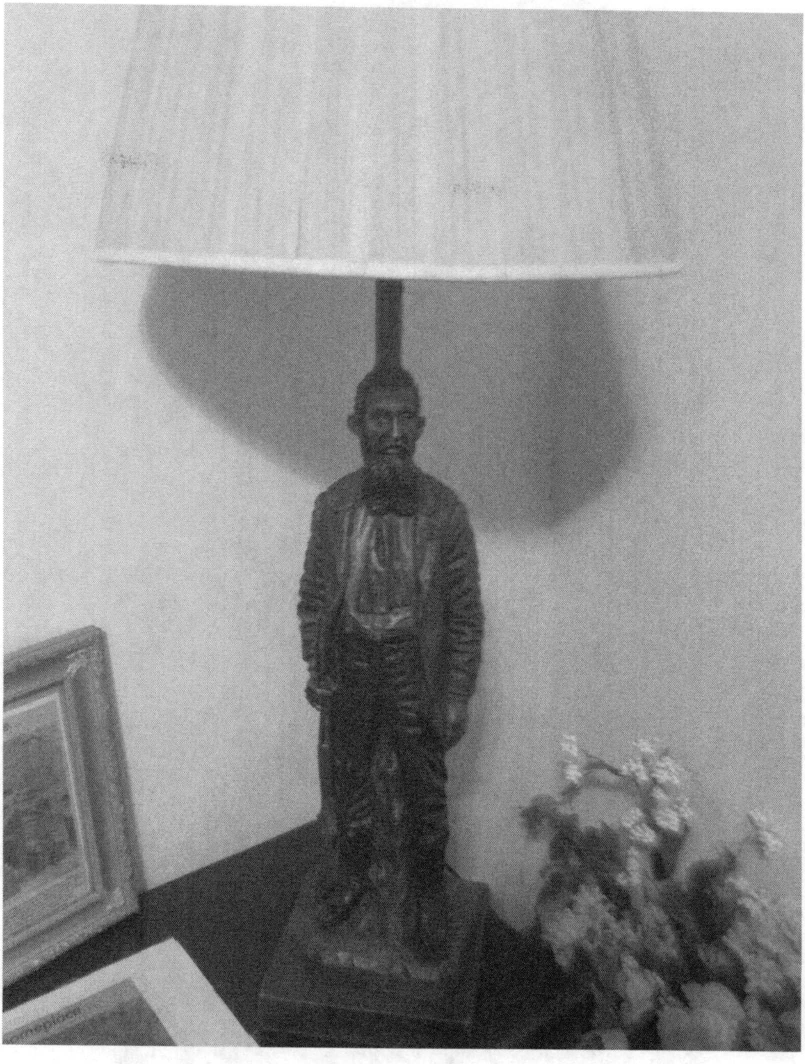

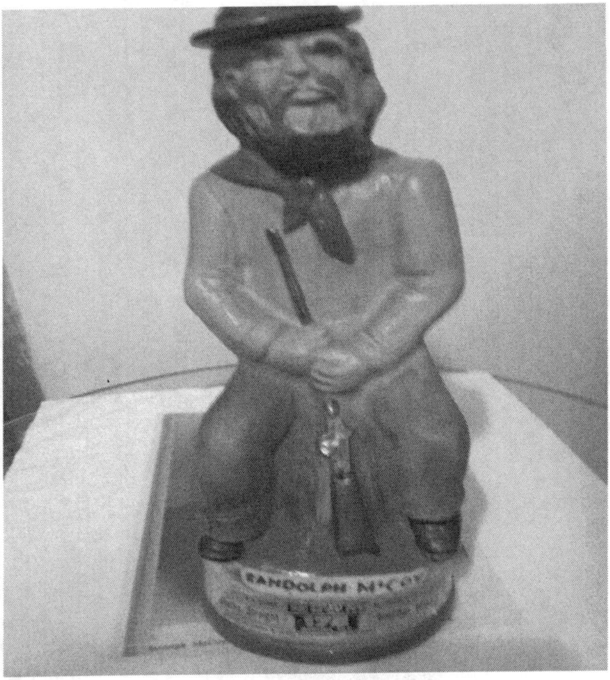

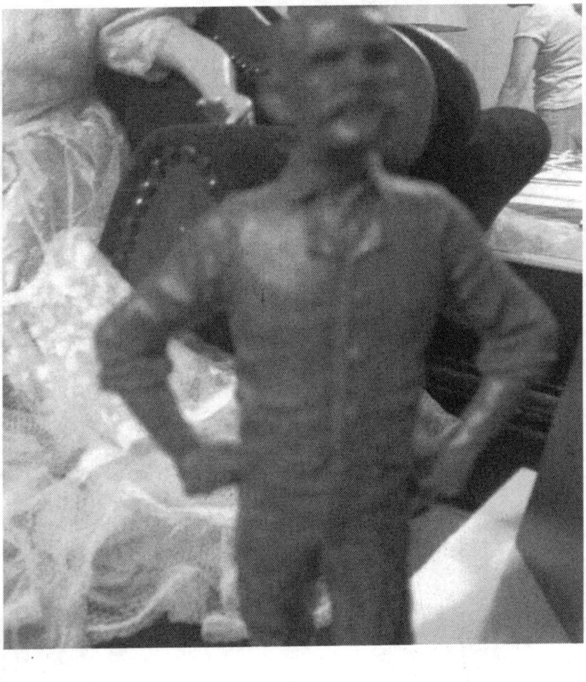

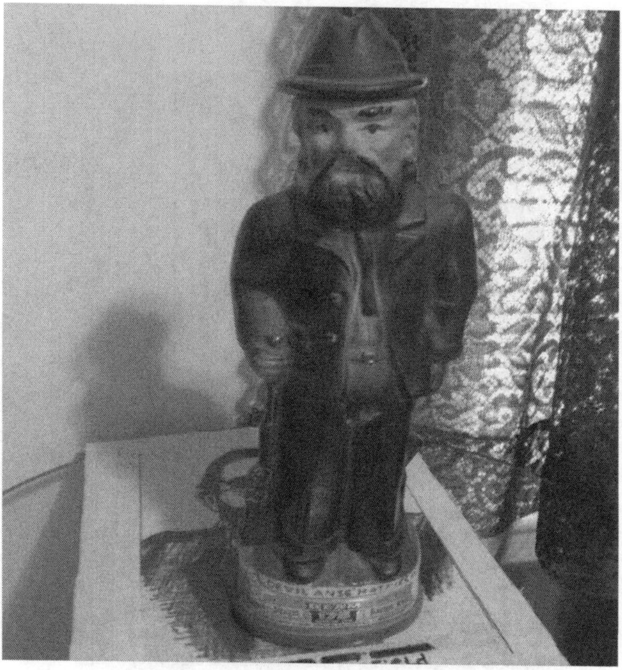

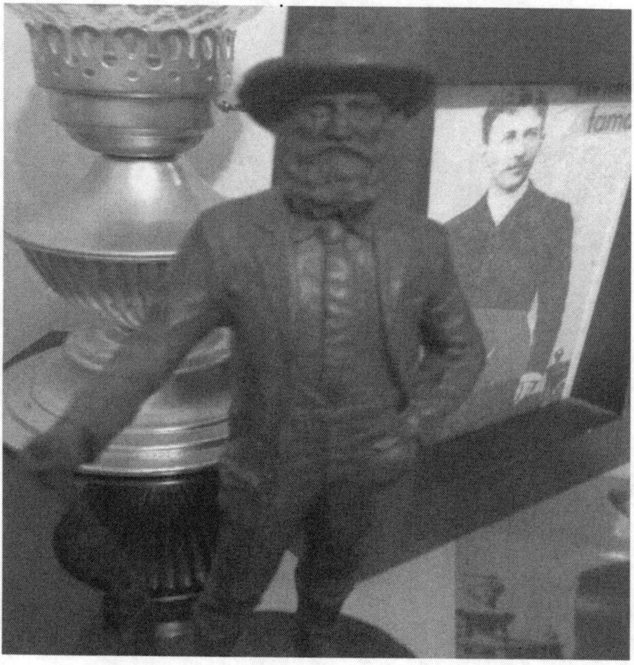

Moms

Ours

~ 244 ~

RANDOLPH McCOY
1825–1914

Famed Feud leader, Randolph McCoy was born on October 30, 1825. He married Sarah McCoy on December 9, 1849. They lost their home and seven children as a result of the Hatfield and McCoy Feud. After the Feud, Randolph operated a ferry in Pikeville for many years. He died on March 28, 1914 and is buried at the Dils Cemetery, Pikeville.

Fred McCoy 1976-77 Jacksonville, Fl. U.S. Marines. Reading Truda McCoy's book the **McCoy's Their Story**.

Have been researching and listening to stories about the feud since I was about 10 years old.

Baby sister Bridgett McCoy in background.

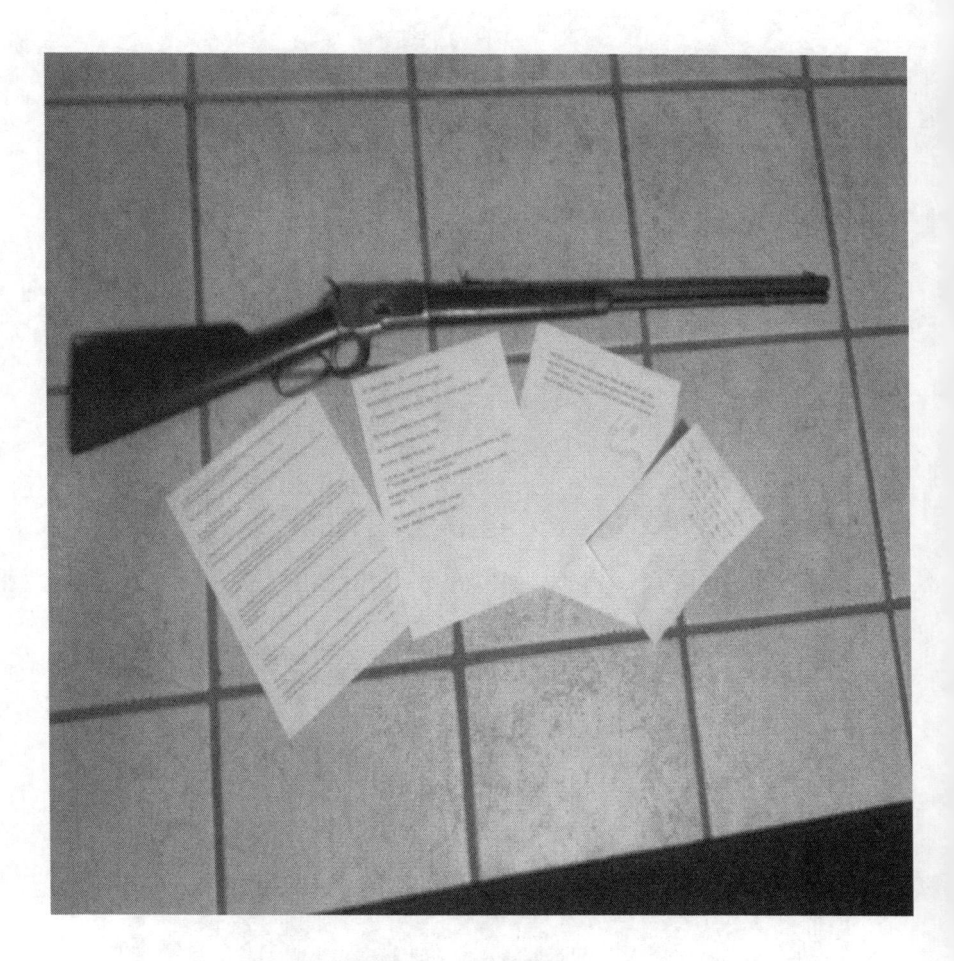

McCoy Rifle

Model 92 Winchester Rifle 32-20 caliber passed down over the last 5 generations.

(Ret.) Det./Police Chief Paul Hatfield and my oldest brother Ricky McCoy

My youngest brother Naaman McCoy and Fred McCoy

Son Bobby Bryant and Fred McCoy

Paris Island 1975

Detective Fred McCoy early 1980's Undercover Narcotics

McCoy's School of Martial Arts

Karate owners and instructors Fred and Barry McCoy

World Record Break 1986

World Record Break 1986

Fred McCoy, lying on a bed of nails with four slabs of concrete weighing 348 pounds. Barry McCoy, smashing concrete with one blow of a 16 pound sledge hammer.

Shelia's parents Jimmy and Rosie Stanley

Fred with grandson Ethan

Daughter, Ella Jane (McCoy) Schuler holding son Ethan, Husband Jimmy Schuler, Shelia and Fred McCoy

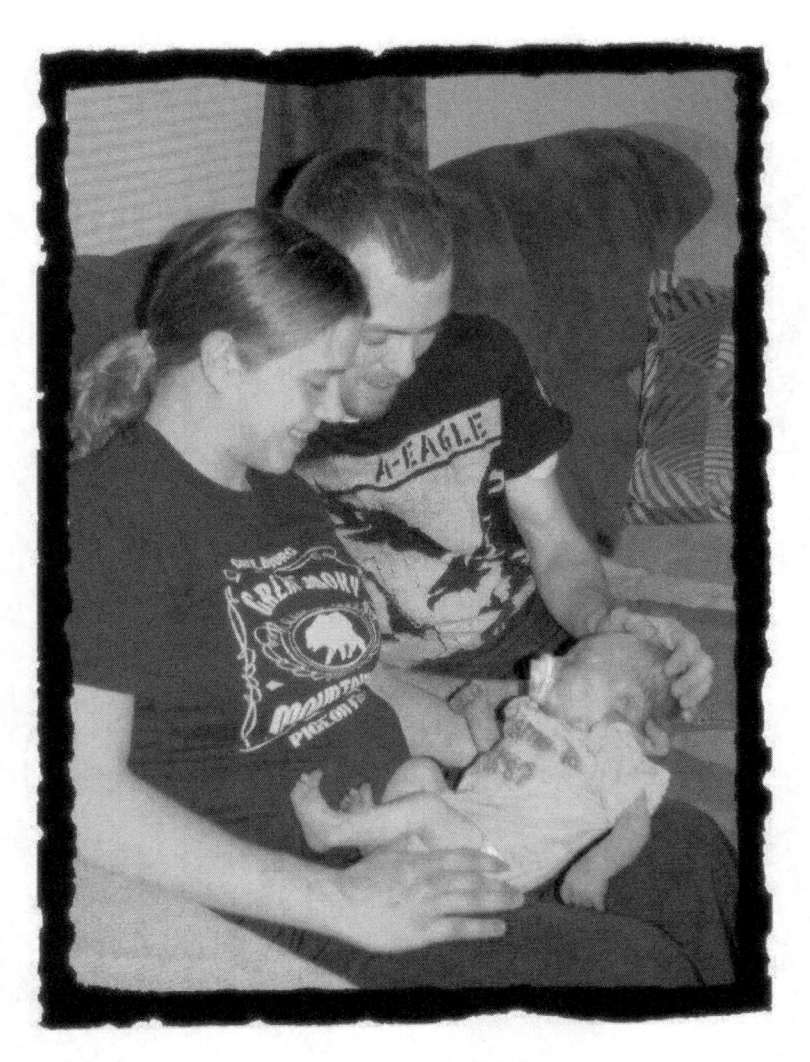

Our Son and Daughter in law

Bobby and Angel (Turpin) McCoy

Along with our Granddaughter Emily Grace.

Cora McCoy my beautiful mother and myself

Dad, myself, Mom

My baby sister Bridgett "McCoy" Martinelli and her family

Our McCoy Family
Bobby Bryant, Shelia, Fred, Ella Jane

The Story of the McCoys

By Barry McCoy

THE FACTS, THE FEUD, THE FURY!

Randolph "Randall" McCoy

Written by a Descendant from both

The Hatfields and McCoys

"My Grandfather was a McCoy and his Mom was Preacher Anderson Hatfields daughter." – Barry McCoy

www.barrymccoy.com

Fred and Shelia
Gatlinburg, Tennessee 2011

Father's Family Name
by Anonymous

You got it from your father
It was all he had to give
So it's yours to use and cherish
For as long as you may live

If you lost the watch he gave you
It can always be replaced;
But a black mark on your name
Can never be erased

It was clean the day you took it
And a worthy name to bear
When he got it from his father
There was no dishonor there

So make sure you guard it wisely
After all is said and done
You'll be glad the name is spotless
When you give it to your son.

Credit/Disclaimer

The Author and Co-Author of this book assumes no responsibilities for the content as being true or false. Most of the stories have been passed down from generation to generation. Bits and pieces were taken from court records and court testimony, books, newspapers, Google, Wikipedia and both the Kentucky and West Virginia Historical Society and various other internet sites.

There is no way to confirm every single story. However, we have made every effort to print the facts on both families. This book is being published as Historical fiction. We did not actually witness any of the feud. We can only rely on our memory, and the memory and stories of our Ancestors.

Book Review

Devil Anse Hatfield Descendent

Best friend and former partner Det./Police Chief (Ret.) Paul Hatfield

Just received my copy of Monument for a Murderer written by Fred and Shelia McCoy. Sat down and read the book this afternoon and really enjoyed the book pics and genealogy. Randal McCoy has always been reflected in a bad light and someone needed to tell the real story of him and his family and what they went thru. Good job Fred and Shelia I hope a lot of people read this and enjoy as much as I did. **Paul Hatfield**

Pike County Tourism

http://www.tourpikecounty.com/index.php?page=hatfields-and-mccoys

Response to: A Complaint

A lady with the last name of Hatfield wrote a pretty harsh letter to me after the release of our first edition. I have edited my response to her and omitted her identity but this was the just of my response needless to say we never received any corrections to any of the stories we had printed in our book.

"We wrote this book for those who want to know the truth. There are a few Hatfields who seem to be upset at what we say in our book. Now, read Hatfields and McCoys by Otis Rice, Blood Feud, by Lisa Alther, The Feuding Hatfields and McCoys by Coleman C. Hatfield, the Tale of the Devil by Coleman Hatfield.

While you are reading these books pretend you are a McCoy. "Get the Picture"? Forget the spelling, the punctuation and grammar. I state on the first few pages, if you are looking for those things to find another book. But, if you want the truth about the feud read on.

What did you find that was not true? That Devil Ance, was not a deserter. That he did not rob and kill under the pretense of being a Logan Wildcat. Or that he did not kill at least one of the three McCoy boys and order the execution of the others.

Were we wrong when we said, "he was a murderer that was never held accountable for his crimes?" Please tell us where we were incorrect so we can correct the inaccuracies before our second addition comes out. We want to print the truth.

When you correct us, please follow up by correcting the Kentucky and West Virginia archives as a lot of our information comes from them. Also, please explain to us why you say that we are not accurate? I even re-printed (with permission) the full statements of Devil Anse, as well as that of Charley Gillespie and Ellison Hatfield. (Who was the son of Ellison Hatfield that was stabbed at the election ground fight). Remember in the other books they printed Randall high tailed it out of the cabin and left his family to perish. Yet in the sworn statements of at least two of the participants that were in fact at the cabin massacre they say the old man shot three of them and was an excellent marksman. Where are our inaccuracies? We used courtroom transcripts/testimony to back up what we say. The other books seem to copy off each other and media reports.

I am sorry I did not please you by keeping that murderer on the pedestal he has been on for so many years. With these ridiculous movies it was time someone spoke up. Please prove us wrong. Please show us what a kind decent man this guy they called the Devil really was. I understand him being somewhat of a mortar to some with the Hatfield name.

But do you have to honor a man that is known for his atrocities and the fear he instilled on others. I see why no one on the McCoys side has ever spoken out about the feud. The truth will be here when we are all gone. The truth is he is not worthy of being labeled a hero, when he was nothing more than a murderer. (Google Life Magazine May 22nd 1944 they acknowledged Devil Anse ordered and set his own Monument before his death) this is no hero but a man that had a serious ego problem.

As far as my poor attempt to being an author I would agree with you, I do not consider myself an author. I do consider myself as someone who stood up, researched and set the record straight for those who really care enough to read it or investigate the truth.

What is shameful is when we know the truth but fail to acknowledge it. Because you would rather brag about the big bear tales from the past.

We wrote a book that is contrary to all the others. Anyone, who is curious read the book, validate the documentation and decide for yourself.

P.S. Nothing against Hatfields just not a fan of the Devil! Please excuse typos, spelling, grammar and punctuations I didn't do very well in English, but it didn't affect my investigative skills."

Like I stated earlier, we never received not even one correction from the lady as to any incorrect information in our 1st edition.

FROM THE FIRST PAGE

Please withhold your judgment and reach no opinion until the last word on the last page of this book is read.

Who won the Feud?

Last page - Last word is...

NOBODY!